Mayflower

·My Story·

Mayflower

The Diary of
Remember Patience Whipple, 1620

By Kathryn Lasky

To today's young immigrants, pilgrims all

While the events described and some of the characters in this book may
be based on actual historical events and real people, Remember Patience
Whipple is a fictional character, created by the author, and her
diary is a work of fiction.

This edition produced for the Book People Ltd,
Hall Wood Avenue, Haydock, St Helens WA11 9UL

First published in the US by Scholastic Inc, 1996
First published in the UK by Scholastic Ltd, 2003

Text copyright © Kathryn Lasky, 1996

ISBN 0 439 95496 7

All rights reserved
Typeset by TW Typesetting, Midsomer Norton, Somerset
Printed and bound by Nørhaven Paperback A/S, Denmark
Cover image: Portrait of a Girl by Anthonie Palamedesz, Private Collection/
Johnny Van Haeften Ltd, London/Bridgeman Art Library
Background image: The Mayflower in Plymouth, Burstein Collection/CORBIS

The right of Kathryn Lasky to be identified as the author of
this work has been asserted by her in accordance with the
Copyright, Designs and Patents Act, 1988.

Mayflower
1620

October 1, 1620. Morning
Mayflower. 1,150 miles sailed

Mem – that's what I answer to. 'Tis short for Remember. My full name being Remember Patience Whipple. Patience was to be my first name, but Mam, my mother, decided it was wrong. I was squally and impatient. They wanted, however, to remember my mother's dear sister who had just passed on. So they slipped the Patience in between. For some it is a good first name, for me it is better as an in-between name. Mam says I am more patient than I once was, but I still have a far way to go. I'm twelve years old. Maybe by the time I am full grown, say fifteen, I shall be patient.

We are journeying to the New World. It is the *Mayflower* that be getting us there, slowly. She measures 90 feet in length and 25 feet in breadth at her broadest point. She is a strong ship but a plodding one, as she creaks her way across this vast grey Atlantic sea.

The reason for our journey is our religion. You see, we are not the Pope's people nor the King's really, but God's people. We are Saints of the Holy Discipline.

"Saints" – for short. That is what all of us English who went to Holland are called. And if we go to this New World, free from old King James and all the fancy church rituals that are not to our way, we can worship as we want. You see, we believe that the church is in our heart and not in a building. So 'tis our hearts that lead us.

But now it is my stomach that is revolting. For days it has been topsy-turvy with me, and the sailing master, Master Jones, says we only have had gales, no real storms. Oh dear, I am feeling pukish. Quissy I call it. I don't want to cast. I don't want to cast. That is all I can think of – vomiting. I must stop writing, dear diary. That sounds so stupid, "dear diary". I must find you a proper name. But I must lay my pen down before I puke all over you...

October 2, 1620
Mayflower

Storm-force winds; too dangerous to go topside to seek out Master Jones for our progress. 'Tis hard to imagine what this New World shall be like. I am used to towns with buildings and winding streets. And people bustling to market and talking Dutch, or English if they be one of us. But the New World is empty of all that. There are no buildings or streets and the only people are feathered men and feathered women and feathered babies, I suppose, who do paint their faces 'tis said, and live in most uncommon shelters.

October 2, 1620. Afternoon
Mayflower

They say we be heading for northern Virginia, near the Hudson River. The King, King James of England, granted the land. Then the merchants formed the company for a plantation where we shall grow things to send back to England to sell.

Too sick to write.

I hate John Billington.

October 3, 1620
Mayflower

Storm still blows.

God forgive my harsh thoughts on John Billington. God Bless John Billington even though I cannot bear him. His brother Francis might be worse.

Mam's got scours, as do so many. There is something in the water or the food that just turns the bowels to liquid. Father took Mam's petticoat topside. Came back drenched but petticoat clean with saltwater scrubbing. Please, dear Lord, I do not want to get the scours and it is not for my vanity … 'tis for my petticoats. I be wearing only two now instead of the usual three, as we had to triple-diaper up my baby sister Blessing when she did get the scours. I'd rather cast than get scours. What a horrid choice. One end or t'other! Oh, dear, the very thought of it does make my innards shiver. I cast now…!

PS Master and Mistress Billington are in the course of a terrible fight. She can screech as loud as the wind. And him with his curses! I don't even know what the fight is about. It does not help my poor knotted guts.

Will Butten, Deacon Fuller's servant, is a clever lad. All the littlest children were carrying on something fierce. Wailing as loud as the storm. He took a pen nib and painted faces on his fingers and then again where his thumb joins his hand. Each face had a name and then he began to tell a story by wiggling his fingers. Soon they all stopped crying. Hummy, my friend, and I think he is quite dear. He also explained to me how the sailing master measures the latitude by peering through his cross-staff at the sun. When the storms cease and we can go topside again, Will promises to show Hummy and me a clever trick for measuring *Mayflower*'s speed.

October 5, 1620
Mayflower

Wind increases. We must take in our sail and drift. I still be feeling poorly.

They call our *Mayflower* a "sweet ship" because she was in the Portuguese wine trade and has not for a long time carried smelly things like fish and tar and turpentine. But she not be so sweet now; not with everyone so close and sick, sleeping below the deck, and with no privies and only buckets. She smells very bad. To think how excited I was when we first boarded this ship. How cosy I found it all, the nooks and crannies. But we are simply too many people, crushed up against one another every hour of the day. The horrible smells, the snores of some of the men, the squalls of the babies. If one wants to change a petticoat with any modesty one must practically crawl into a barrel. The men are less modest than the women. Often they pull off their shirts and I see their backs and stomachs. I try to look away, but sometimes it is impossible and I have discovered that some men have

13

hair on their backs! Is that not peculiar?

How I wish they would let me go topside for a breath of air. It has been days since I have seen a drop of sunlight. But it is forbidden for the children to go onto the upper deck what with the pitching and rolling and the waves thrashing and crashing. And if we didn't fall over, one of the sailors might throw us over. They hate us Saints and they make fun of our sickness. They call us "puke-stockings". They are as rude as the Billington boys. By the way, I am sure Francis Billington pinched one of my biscuits.

October 7, 1620
Mayflower, 1,420 miles sailed

CAST
SPEW
SPOUT
PUKE

Hummy Sawyer and I are making a list of all the words for these wrathful contortions of our innards. It makes us feel better. And speaking of words I must think of a name for you, dear…? But I feel so poorly now 'tis all I can do to write.

October 9, 1620
Mayflower

The gales have pushed us back twenty miles! We are practically back to where we were yesterday! I am most depressed. This wind is indeed like a big fist in our face. Father says the ship cannot go against it when the wind be square on! Agony!

October 10, 1620
Mayflower. 1,560 miles sailed

I write now with trembling hand. A most horrendous thing has happened. There was what they call a rogue wave that rose out of the storm seas. It felt as if our poor little ship was flying for endless seconds and then there was a terrible crack. Yes, indeed we have cracked the main beam! It surely buckled and now the deck above us is like a sieve and we are all drenched. All the men came together. All so grim-faced. And then 'twas my own father who perhaps has solved the problem, for he remembered the immense iron screw we brought from Holland for building our village in the New World.

If it does not work, our ship will founder and sink. I try to imagine drowning in this snarling sea. If indeed it comes to that, if the ship goes down, I would hope I would be drowned before a shark would eat me. Sharks are a very bad sign when following a ship. I saw some one day when it was calmer and I was still sick, casting over the side. They probably have my scent now. They'll come right for me. I must not have these dark thoughts. I must have faith in God and man. These men, my father, the carpenter, the sailing master, Master Bradford, Elder Brewster, they will figure out something. We all pray that 'tis possible to raise the broken beam back into place and then with a post under it, secure it once it is mended.

October 12, 1620
Mayflower. 1,790 miles sailed

It has worked. God's providence has come down on our little ship. The main beam is raised and repaired! We are blessed. Last evening we assembled for prayers of thanks. Soon after that the winds abated and the rigging became quiet for the first time in nearly two weeks. We could hear to think, hear to pray, hear to listen to each other. And Hummy and I chattered all through the night.

Hummy and I are going to put up a real fuss to sleep in the shallop now. The shallop is a small boat to be

17

used for exploring the coast when we finally get there. It is perhaps twenty feet long and of shallow draft and is stowed in the tween decks. We need just a little place for ourselves. It would be a change of scenery. I am so sick of staring at those pegs and those planks where I have been sleeping and I am so tired of hearing the snores of Master and Mistress Billington and seeing his hairy back. I would imagine that the smells would not be better but maybe they would at least be different smells! Will Butten says that the best place is where he often goes – the longboat on deck. But I doubt Mam would let me go out there in the night air. The vapours you know. She is most fearful of night air, especially when the wind comes from the south.

October 13, 1620
Mayflower. 1,805 miles sailed

Last evening Mam was able to cook over the charcoal brazier for the first time in days. We had a nice supper. It was a flesh day so we could have meat. We did, salt beef with mustard and vinegar, peas, ship biscuit, and Blessing had her favourite: warmed-up oatmeal. I would love a bag pudding or some frumenty, the kind Mam makes all thick and full of cinnamon. It drips off your spoon so nice and warm. But that we shall have to wait a long time for.

In any case, it is a fine day now. The grey skies have washed away leaving this immense blue bowl over our heads. We have fresh, steady winds, northeasterlies. The monkeys, as they call the sailors who scramble up the masts, were in the rigging and every piece of canvas has been shaken out. *Mayflower* looks like a many-winged bird with her fore and main courses flying, and the topsails swelling against the sky!

We are allowed topside and I do not feel sick any more, not one speck of the quissies. We set ourselves in earnest now for the New World! And not only is the ship's course set, but I feel that I, too, can begin in earnest with my diary. I have a name for you now. But first you must know your history – how you came to be. I shall write that down tomorrow. For now I want to enjoy the fresh breezes.

As promised, here is your story, which began in Holland.

When we were in Holland, and safe from King James, our Ruling Elder, William Brewster, two or more years ago, began to print church books that spoke out harshly against King James and the Bishops. These books had to be printed in secret for it would be most dangerous if it were found out. My mother and father were among the very few who did know.

You see, there came to be a problem with the press, something broke and they asked for my father to help, he being so clever with carpentry and fixing things. My father was given some batches of paper by these people, perhaps as payment for his work. I am not sure. Mam, however, cut them up and stitched them together. With some scraps of leather she got from a cobbler on Rozengracht street she made a cover. Using an awl she pressed my first name into the cover in a most delicate and pretty manner.

That all seems so long ago now. As I sit here in the sliding shadows and putrid smells of this ship 'tis hard for me to believe that there was ever a Rozengracht street, or for that matter a place called Holland. Will and Hummy can scarce believe the stories I tell them about skating on the canals. One must be careful of course when going under a bridge, I explain, as that is where the ice can be the thinnest, especially around the pilings.

I wander off to Holland in my thoughts more and more but I must finish the story as to how you came into my hands. Mam did not give me the book until we were well clear of England and truly off for the New World. I do believe that she was fearful that King James or his men would somehow trace this paper to our family, throw us into jail, and cut us into pieces. For it was said that he had sworn vengeance on anyone connected with the books.

So she waited till Land's End was but a sketchy line behind us. And then she gave you to me and told me that this was to be my diary. That I must live up to my name and Remember, not just for my own sake but for my children's and my children's children and their children's children. Mam said to me, "This book is to be like your closest friend." Then she paused and said,

"No, 'tis closer than your closest friend, 'tis like another part of you, a true and real part of you."

If you be like another part of me, then you should share my name. And if that part be a true and real part, it would be false to call you Patience. It would be more honest and real to call you Impatience – and for short I think 'tis best we settle on Imp – so dear Imp, this is your name.

Yours, Mem

October 16, 1620
Mayflower. 1,840 miles sailed

Dear Imp,

I want to tell you about Hummy and all the others as well. Hummy is short for Humility. Humility Sawyer. Hummy is exactly my age. She was born on the very same day, August 23, 1608! Now we have been trying to find out what hour. Mam told me that I was born just after midnight on that day. Hummy's mother died shortly before the voyage began so we cannot ask her – and her father, poor soul, is so melancholy of his wife's death that we dare not say anything to remind him of her. So 'tis a mystery, the hour of Hummy's birth.

But is it not as if we were destined to be best friends? There are other things to bond us as well. We both hate spinning and stitchery. We both dared show each other our samplers, and they are both the most horrid messes one can ever imagine. We both love words and to play with them like the time we made a list of all the ways to say cast. And most fun of all we have made up nicknames for nearly all the people on the ship.

Our favourite is Commander Shrimp for Captain Myles Standish, because he is so florid in colour and with his bright red hair and small stature he reminded us so of a shrimp.

Hummy and I had never met before we arrived in Southampton. That is where she joined the ship. Hummy is not a Saint. She be what we call a "Stranger". That is our name for those who are not part of the Saints of The Holy Discipline. We also be called Separatists because we separated from the Church of England. Myles Standish is a Stranger, too, and so is John Alden and the Mullinses and the dreadful Billingtons, though I hate to mention that

23

family with the rest of these souls. For although these people be Strangers they be good folk I believe, except with the possibility of the Billingtons.

In all we are 102 passengers, with just over 40 of us Saints from Leyden. The rest be a few Saints and Strangers from London and parts of England to the south. The Strangers, like Hummy's father Richard Sawyer, did not come for religion, but for a chance to make a better living.

My own dear mother and father came for all good reasons: first and foremost, religion. In Holland, Sabbath was becoming a sore pain to my parents. For indeed, the Dutch thought of it as a day of pleasure – "unbridled frolicking" were Mam's words. Oh, they went to church but then they played. Children went about rolling hoops and howling and turning cartwheels.

In the winter they would have skating races on the canals on the Sabbath day! And it wasn't just the Sabbath that was the problem. When an English girl who lived right down the street from us married a Dutch boy, well, my parents were shocked most awfully.

But the one single thing that really made up my parents' minds about leaving Holland was Blessing, my baby sister. She is just two and one half now, but about six months ago when she was two or a bit under, guess what her first words after "mama" were. "dank-u," which means "thank you" in Dutch. Mam had handed her some bread smeared with honey, and Blessing reached out with her little chubby hand and said, "Dank-u, Mama." Well, that was it. You would have thought our dear little Blessing had spoke a curse. Mam nearly fainted. And I remember looking at mother as she stared at this little baby. It was all written right there on her face – visions of her children marrying Dutchmen, going to churches with organ music, giving birth to little bishops or something.

It was only a few short months later we sailed for England and here we be. And we are not just Saints and not just Strangers but I better like the word Master William Bradford did make for us. We all are pilgrims. Two nights ago he used that word when he offered a prayer of thanksgiving for the successful repair of the beam. He said, "Although we have our differences, we are all God's children and as such we be but specks in the vastness of this ocean, but precious unto our Lord and now together we are voyagers, pilgrims, and look to Thine infinite mercy and providence."

I like the thought of Hummy and myself, no longer

just being Saint and Stranger. For those two words doth pull us apart. 'Tis better to find a word that brings us together and might fit us both. And the word that does that is pilgrim.

That is all for now, Imp. I must go help Mam with Blessing.

Love, Mem

PS Did I tell you that Hummy has such a dear little face? Her hair is slightly red, like cinnamon. And she has round little cheeks and a round little chin. It is as if she is made all from circles and then sprinkled with freckles.

Later the same day

Dear Imp,

I have to write to you twice today. I am almost incredulous, but my gentle mam came close to losing her temper with Elder Brewster. For some time Mam has been complaining to Father that she thinks William Brewster is too vivid in his language when he describes the horrors of King James and his awful Bishops.

Now this evening we were having our supper down below – just finishing a few bites of salt horse and the hardtack when the Brewsters' young son asked his father some question and it makes William Brewster remember his dear friends from his college days, who were indeed killed by the Bishops for wanting to make the church pure.

"How were they killed?" the boy asked.

"Hanged and worse," Elder Brewster replied darkly. I felt Mam, who was sitting beside me, flinch.

"They were first thrown in jail for a long long time and left in filth and half starved to rot. Then they were brought out to be hanged."

"And...?" said the Brewster child. All the other children were leaning forward to listen but Mam just seemed almost frozen beside me, despite Blessing wriggling in her lap.

"And..." He spoke slowly. "Just when they had a few breaths of life still in them, they were cut down. Their bellies were cut open, their guts drawn out and burning coals put in their bowels! That is what the bishops do. Mere killing is not enough."

Well, Mam, who had been sitting still as a stone, suddenly jumped up with Blessing in her arms.

"Elder Brewster." She spoke through clenched

teeth. "This is not conversation for children nor for anyone sitting at the table of the Lord partaking in the nourishment He hath provided. We do not want our children's sleep to be troubled with nightmares."

One could have heard a pin drop despite the creaking and moaning of the ship's timbers. William Brewster jumped up and glared at Mother. But I saw John Alden smiling gently at her, and then I saw Commander Shrimp give a fierce look toward Elder Brewster. And I tell you the Shrimp tells some pretty strong stories himself.

I think Mam spoke truthfully in what she said. I was proud of her, but it is most uncommon, unheard of, for a woman to speak out thusly. And it disturbed me the way Elder Brewster glared at her, for after all he is the Ruling Elder of the Green Gate Congregation from which we all come in Leyden. It does frighten me, and now maybe instead of the nightmares about how they did hang and quarter those men I might be having others. I shall not forget, Imp, the glare in his eye, and how my mother did not flinch one bit, but boldly met his eyes.

Good night, Imp.

Love again, Mem

Dear Imp,

It is starting to blow fierce again, but so far I feel not a twinge of the quissies. Captain Standish said I looked "pert" when several others were casting and I was trying to help out. I do think that perhaps at last both Hummy and I are used to the roll and the violent pitches, for she is feeling quite fit, too. Master Jones says that we've both got our "sea legs" now. Master Jones is very nice, but the rest of the crew are most awful. In particular there is one especially profane sailor. He is the one who calls us puke-stockings and goes about bullying all the Saints and making fun of our prayers, cursing us to kingdom come. He speaks often of throwing half of us overboard. And then there is the foul-mouthed old bo'sun. He be not condemning us, but the mighty oaths he does roar at the monkeys in the rigging!! Enough to make your ears bleed, says Will Butten. As awful as these sailors be, I cannot imagine, however, having to go up into the rigging in these gale-force winds to shorten sail.

29

Hummy and I and Will B peeked out of a hatch and watched two sailors go up to haul in the topsails. 'Tis a scarifying sight, I tell you, as we watched for they must swing into the ratlines between the rigging. The ratlines are like rope ladders – then they climb hand over hand to the topsail yard. And once there comes the worst part of all for they have to swing out on to the footropes to start adjusting the sails. There is nothing between them and death but air, a few ropes, and howling wind. They must do this in blizzards and rain and often in the pitch-black of night. There they were holding on for dear life, yet trying to work at the same time, high above the deck of this wildly pitching ship. They could have been flung from the rigging into the deep at any moment.

Hummy and I didn't know a topsail from a mizzen when we first came aboard. But Will, he knows everything there is to know about sailing ships.

It must be admitted 'tis not an easy life these sailors have. Still they should be nicer to us and not cheer every time we puke. Yes, they often do that!!

'Tis hard to write with all this pitching. But I should tell you a bit about Will Butten. He is Deacon Samuel Fuller's servant. Deacon Fuller is also our surgeon and he does much cutting and bleeding and Will helps him with it. But Will says it does give him the quissies and he has to fight to keep his eyes open because he cannot stand the sight of blood. Hummy and I think he is the best and most clever boy. Always a cheerful word and often times he helps the women with the babies. He has a gentle and calm way about him and he knows ever so many finger games that he plays with the babies. Blessing just takes to him so. He be a few years older than Hummy and me, but we all like the same things and he likes our word games and especially the nicknames we think up. One last word before I stop: guess who the Bilgewaters, or the Bilges as we sometimes call them, are? Tomorrow I shall reveal their true identity.

Love, Mem

October 18, 1620
Mayflower. 1,900 miles sailed

Dear Imp,

There is a lull in the storm so I write, but I do not believe the storm is over. There was too much fury for it to blow itself out so quickly.

31

The Bilgewaters – as promised: William Bradford told my father they are the profanest of families he has ever encountered. The children are as unruly and nasty as they come. They snitch and they bedevil the two dogs on board – well, not the big mastiff, but the spaniel that belongs to one passenger. Hummy and I are just waiting for them to get bit. You can tell something of character about children who mistreat dogs. That was our first clue about the Bilge children. And then they always are trying to peek where they shouldn't – including under our petticoats. Hummy and I were sitting on some barrels the other day just dangling our feet when John Alden came along to check on the barrels and then he suddenly yanks up little Francis who had been hiding under some rope and canvas just by the barrels staring right up our dresses. John Alden gave him a good cuff. I hear the wind coming round again. I'll write fast now.

There are 30 children in all, the youngest is an infant. Some are from England and some are Saints like us from Holland. Some like Will Butten and the More children are orphans and travel as servants for other families. There is also Priscilla Mullins but she be eighteen. Not really a child, however Hummy and I love Priscilla and think she is a most beautiful girl. We call her Lark, short for larkspur because that is our favourite flower and she has very blue eyes.

There be one child that I wish dearly was on board, and that is the son of William and Dorothy Bradford. His parents feared too much for his safety on this crossing and plan to send for him later. There is not a soul aboard the vessel who, when we were departing from Holland for Southampton, did not have their hearts seared by the terrible and frightening cries coming from that child on the pier as he saw his mother and father pull away in the ship. Nor will anyone ever forget the grief carved so deeply in Dorothy Bradford's face. She has hardly spoken a word for this entire passage and appears more melancholy than Hummy's father. I do not know what I should have done if Mother and Father had left me and Blessing behind. I would think I should rather die.

Must stop now. Storm back with full force – but no quissies.

Love, Mem

October 21, 1620
Mayflower

Dear Imp,

The Lord giveth … the Lord taketh, then He giveth and taketh back again. 'Tis the best way to sum up the last day as this storm still rages. First, John Howland was swept overboard. He came topside and was scrubbed right off the deck. 'Twas several minutes before he was hauled in with a boat hook but the sailing master reported that he went under the water some fathoms during the course. The Lord, however, gave him back to us! And just whilst he was swirling in those crashing waves, Mistress Hopkins collapsed and has gone into labour, her child coming early. She moaned through the night but she came forth with a jolly little baby boy who looks none the worse for wear, having been born between the gasps of a raging gale. I, for one, found his squalls most pleasant after the shrieks of the storm.

During this time that very proud and profanest of the sailors, the one who called us all "puke-stocking" began indeed himself to cast blood. Towards morning of this day he died and the men took his body topside and slid him over the rails. Is it not odd that the man who threatened to throw half of us overboard is in fact the first to go?

I wonder what they shall name the new babe?

Good night.

Love, Mem

October 23, 1620
Mayflower. 2,160 miles sailed

Dear Imp,

Master and Mistress Hopkins have decided to name the baby Oceanus. I think it is a good name, but I am not sure that had I been born on board this ship I might not have preferred the name Atlanticus. Atlanticus has the sound of the storm waves that crash against the hull. And this infant was born not in a lull, but within the heart of a full Atlantic gale. And he be crying like fury as I write.

Love, Mem

October 24, 1620
Mayflower. 2,210 miles sailed

D_{ear} Imp,

The storm is blowing itself out, but I am occupied with many unsettled feelings and worries about sundry things. Perhaps if I make a list it will help. I do not like the shadows of fears lurking about. I shall bring them into the light.

1) I did not like the way Elder Brewster looked at Mam as she prepared our supper over the coals tonight. I believe he is still angry with her for telling him to mind his tongue.

2) Hummy's father, Master Sawyer, grows more melancholy by the day. This is very hard on Hummy. He never speaks to her and I am sure she be missing her mother as much as he.

3) Dear Will B is looking quite poorly and when I walked by him I found him sleeping at this unusual hour and looking quite feverish.

There that be a list of my worries.

Love, Mem

October 27, 1620
Mayflower. 2,340 miles sailed

Dear Imp,

Will B appears truly not well at all and Hummy and I cannot understand why Deacon Fuller does not give him more attention. We fetch him water and try to get a piece of biscuit or a bite of oatmeal down him. Sometimes he is near delirious and calling out for his Mam. Now think you not the Fullers could take a little more time with him as he is their servant? Not that Hummy or I mind. But we are doing all we can and it seems not enough. After all, the Deacon Fuller is a doctor and they are the upgrowns. I told Hummy that I am going to go to Deacon and ask for a draught for Will to ease his sleep and these terrible nightmare deliriums that seem to seize him.

Love, Mem

October 28, 1620
Mayflower. 2,400 miles sailed

Dear Imp,

I am so mad I could boil. I went to Deacon Fuller
and asked for a draught for Will B and he says he only
has a bit left and cannot spare it save for an
emergency. This *is* an emergency, I think, but I dare
not say it for I know children must not back talk. So
I just whisper, in a small little voice that I am not
proud of, "Well, Will is fiercely sick and does have
most awful visions in his fevers."

And guess what that horrid man says to me?
"Profane visions are the result of a profane life. Hast
nothing to do with the fever." I be stunned. He had
treated that terrible sailor who had died a few days
before. Was he comparing our dear Will to that man
who had called down curses upon all of us,
threatening in fact to throw us overboard? I am
silent, but I think to myself. Maybe this man who is
a Deacon and a surgeon is really nothing more than
a butcher. And I know this for certain: Will Butten

38

is not a profane being and his deliriums ride on his fever and nought else.

Love, Mem

October 30, 1620
Mayflower. 2,530 miles sailed

Dear Imp,

This is the very darkest thing I have ever told you, only you I can trust. Hummy and I have decided that if Will has not improved by tonight we are going to steal the draught. It is the most awful thing watching Will. He hardly recognizes either Hummy or myself. He seems so alone in his terror.

Love, Mem

October 31, 1620
Mayflower

Dear Imp,

Well, thank the Lord we did not have to steal the draught. There be another surgeon doctor on this ship, not a Saint, mind you, and one that we have not paid any heed to. His name is Giles Heale. But he, having passed by poor Will's pallet many times, became increasingly concerned. I watched him. So at last I went up and asked if he indeed had some of the draught to ease Will's feverish dreams. Hummy could hardly believe it, because she knew that we Saints seemed to avoid him and she told me later that indeed Elder Brewster did look oddly at me when he saw me speaking to Giles Heale. But the good physician said that he most certainly did and had thought that most naturally Deacon Fuller would have dosed him. When I told him nay, he immediately fetched his satchel.

Then, would you believe it, Imp? The old Deacon comes up and says, "What are you doing to the boy? That is my patient." And Giles Heale just as calm as anything says, "I am doing what should have been done two days ago, Sir. I am giving this boy a draught before his fever burns a hole into his brain." For all the Deacon's pious ways and all his pompous views, this simple Stranger knew the true path better. I love the notion that the good man's name is what he tries to do – Heale.

Love, Mem

November 4, 1620
Mayflower

Dear Imp,

I am not so sure about Will. He only squeezed my hand once today and not at all for Hummy. I can think of nothing except poor Will. This voyage goes on too long, but if it would mean his life would be spared it could go on forever.

Love, Mem

November 5, 1620
Mayflower

Dear Imp,

It has been days since either Hummy or I have been topside, so I have no idea of the progress we make. Our world has shrunk totally to the circumference of Will's pallet. We eat beside him, what little we care to eat; we sleep beside him. I know his face so well. I know every thin little blue vein in his fluttering eyelids. I know how his dark blond hair sweeps in a reverse S shape back from his temples.

Love, Mem

November 6, 1620
Mayflower. 2,800 miles sailed

Dear Imp,

Will died a few minutes past midnight this night.
Love, Mem

November 6, 1620. Written at dawn
Mayflower. 2,835 miles sailed

Dear Imp,

43 North, and 2,835 miles from England. I shall
never forget those numbers. That is where Will is.
That is where they slipped his poor body over the side.
Had we flowers, Hummy and I would have tossed
them over to mark the spot. But we had none so we
took a knife to the hems of each one of our extra
dresses, mine be red and Hummy's be blue. We cut

43

strips from them and then when Lark saw what we were doing, she right there and then sat down and took the knife to her own dress, the very one that she was wearing. With these strips we braided a colourful braid with some white from our most under petticoats. And so when they took Will topside to slip him over, as the prayers were being spoken, Hummy and I together tossed the braid into the sea just as the water closed over dear Will Butten's head.

Hummy and I did not want to go below. We could not face that rank dark space any more, not with its close air and then the constant fighting of the Billingtons; and the very presence of Deacon Fuller will forever unnerve me. But most of all we felt that we had to stand our watch over Will. We had to watch that ocean to which he now belonged. We had to see him through his first night of eternity on this vast and endless sea.

That is all, dear Imp. I feel a great desolation. I must fight for my faith now; my faith that although Will Butten seemed in this world so alone that he be in another now joined forever with something of comfort and love.

Mam came up with biscuits and salt beef for me and Hummy. Salt beef! And it not being a flesh day. You see how discomposed we all are! But Mam seems to understand our need to be up here and she touched each of our faces – her hand lingering a bit on Hummy's as if she felt perhaps she needed a bit extra since her father is so melancholy. She said to us that we might sleep from now on in the longboat topside as long as the weather holds and there are no storms. That she will fix us a bed warmer with live coals wrapped in a tinderbox and give us extra coverings. That is some solace. But even better solace would be the sight of land. It has been so long. We must be getting near. At least that is what the sailors say.

Love, Mem

November 7, 1620
Mayflower. 2,850 miles sailed

Dear Imp,

The Bilgewater boys are in real trouble now. They tried to drown the ship's cat in a barrel of water. They claimed that they were just giving it a bath or some nonsense about teaching it to swim. Master Jones thrashed them! He said that cat is worth the two of them together and if we don't have a good cat aboard rats will take us over. So he is making the boys each catch a rat a day until the end of the voyage. He says that he believes that the punishment should fit the crime. It does disturb me, however, to think of those boys stalking rats, because I have a feeling in my bones that they will do some sort of mischief with them.

Love, Mem

November 8, 1620
Mayflower. 2,900 miles sailed

Dear Imp,

Hummy and I love sleeping in the longboat on deck. It is so much fresher than below, and all the sounds are different. The first night after Will died and we slept here, we just huddled together, holding on to each other, and cried. I kept thinking of all those little faces he drew so cunningly on his hands. I wondered how long would they last in the seawater and if a fish might come up and find a story in Will Butten's fingers. So silly but it made me feel good thinking about Will cajoling the fish as he once had the babies.

I feel that I have entered an entirely new world up here in the longboat, and, oddly enough, I feel much closer to Will B, for this is where he slept and now I know how he knew so much about the ship and its sailing.

The longboat is stowed just behind the forecastle under the crow's nest, where the lookout stands watch. But we have a good view of all. It is on the upper deck that the crew lives and where their cook has his own galley. It is on the poop deck that the sailing master's stateroom is, but he has kindly shared this cabin and the ship's officers' cabins in steerage with some of the more important people such as Elder Brewster and his wife and the Bradfords.

But the very most important people at that end of the ship are the helmsman and the officer on deck. 'Tis the helmsman who steers the ship. The helmsman, however, cannot see where he is going from his position. 'Tis the officer on deck who keeps a sharp eye on the compass and sings out the directions to the helmsman. So all through the night the darkness is laced with these lovely words, that are orders – "starboard a little," "full-and-by," "luff her a little," "steady now."

And now in addition to these wonderful words Hummy and I can clearly hear the ring of the bells, signalling the change of watches.

The best part, however, about sleeping out is the dawn. That first morning after Will died it came up pink and grey with a touch of blue. Indeed it seemed almost as if those strips of cloth we braided for Will had floated up yonder into the sky and braided together the clouds.

Love, Mem

November 9, 1620
Mayflower. 2,950 miles sailed

Dear Imp,

"Land ahoy!" The call from the crow's nest cracked the dawn. Hummy's and my eyes flew open. I sat up so quick I banged my head and have an egg agrowing on my brow. But we all hurried out. Unable to believe the words, our eyes wide in the half-light of dawn. Several of us crowded along the rail. The sailors saw it first, the faint dark line against the horizon. Their eyes be trained to pick out such features from the unending plainness of the sea and sky. But within minutes of searching the horizon with our eyes, Hummy and I began to see the same.

We held each other's hands so tightly and almost dared not breathe, but minute by minute the line became firmer and began to thicken. 'Twas not a wisp of a dream but real. It had taken us all of 65 days but finally we are here. This be the New World and it doth fill my eyes for the first time. My eyes did blur with tears, and Hummy and I turned and hugged each other so hard and both thought of our dear Will, lying at the bottom of this sea. But Hummy did whisper to me, "Mem, he now be in heaven and his eyes doth reflect the glory of the Lord, and he sits with his mother once again."

And these words of Hummy's did help us both and we turned to look once more on this New World at the far edge of this vast and terrible sea.

Love, Mem

The New World

Dear Imp,

I begin now this second part of our diary, even though it is the same day. I consider the voyage finished and this be the New World part. Though I must tell you we have been well surprised here. This is not northern Virginia, and the Hudson River is nowhere near. Master Jones felt it might be no more than ten leagues or more to the south of this latitude. No, we seemed to have missed northern Virginia and have sailed to a place known as Cape Cod. The sailing master but a few hours before, when he was still set on heading south, brought *Mayflower* perilously close to some dangerous shoal water. The tides ripped fiercely across the shallows and the current was against us. The wind was dying and darkness coming on. We could hear the roar of the breakers and it was most frightening. The sailing master and John Carver, Master Bradford, and my father and the first mate were called in to discuss what should be done. It was decided that the danger of becoming trapped in the shoals and the breaking waves was indeed too great and that we must forget notions of the Hudson River. So we turned around, sailed back to Cape Cod Bay and dropped anchor.

Father took me and Hummy to the Round House, which is where all the sea charts are kept and the courses are plotted. First Mate Clark showed us a map of this part of the New World coastline that was drawn by Captain John Smith on his voyage six years ago in 1614. At that time Smith had made a voyage up the coast from northern Virginia and called this region New England. Cape Cod had been named by sailors because of all the fish that abound in these waters. It hangs out into the waters embracing the bay like a very long skinny arm. Now we are in the crook of the elbow, it feels most cosy and we ride easy on our anchor and the moonlight falls through the clouds like streams of silver. And all through the night Hummy and I whisper in heated voices: "We are in the New World. This be the New World!"

Good night, Imp.

Love from the New World, Mem

November 10, 1620
Cape Cod Bay

Dear Imp,

I am writing this just as I watch – a pod of whales! They frolic gently around our ship. They are not the large ones that we have heard about, but are considered rather small, no more than twenty feet in length. They blow through their spout holes, they dive, they roll over sometimes as if to cock an eye at us and get a better look. One came especially close to us, rolled, and looked right at me. I peered back closely and found the eye, in its deep folds of skin, to possess an intelligence, to in fact have a remarkably human-like aspect to it and be not at all fish-like.

The weather is clear and cold. We have nestled further into the crook of the elbow and can see white sand dunes and then gentle hills rising behind them. There is, of course, much talk of feathered men. Myles Standish and Elder Brewster spend a considerable amount of time planning for defences against them. The tales can grow quite wild. But the notion of the feathered men does not bother me as much as some of the squabbling below. Hummy just went below to fetch something and came back to report a furious row going on between the Saints from Leyden and some of the Strangers.

Later the same day

Mam just came up from below with Blessing, saying she could not stand the "growling". She spoke of a mutiny! How could we have got this far to have fights break out now? But it seems that since our sailing master's rather large navigational error, which put us here instead of northern Virginia, we are outside the region governed by the patent that was granted us. This, according to Mam, means we are outside the law in some sense as soon as we disembark. And there are those amongst the Strangers who no longer want to be part of our community, but to have free licence. These rebel Strangers were saying that here in New England none has power to command them.

But this, Mam says, would be a most dreadful consequence. For in such a wild and savage land we must work together for the good of all. She says that William Bradford is presently below making a most impassioned speech and scribbling on papers some sort of letter or statement of agreement that might please all parties in some way. She says it appears to her a very difficult, nearly impossible, task but she trusts Master Bradford.

I want desperately to go ashore, but Mam says I can wager that there will be no going ashore until this is thrashed out and settled.

No more to write, Imp. Let us hope that with God's help these men, Saints and Strangers, will find the way.

Love, Mem

November 11, 1620
Cape Cod Harbour

Dear Imp,

God Bless Master Bradford. He has drawn the men into accord. They have signed a form called a compact, The Mayflower Compact, in which it is agreed that all the people, Saints and Strangers alike, shall combine into one body or company and submit to one government with a governor to be chosen. Then they went on and chose John Carver for the governor. I do not know why they did not choose Bradford, but Carver is a good man.

With that settled the men can begin to go ashore and explore. I am so proud. My dear father has been chosen to go with this first landing party. There be sixteen men who set out now well armed to fetch some wood and look about on the land. The Bilgewater boys are furious. They wanted to go. We are of course all anxious to get off the ship and have a look for ourselves. I am so excited to hear what father shall report. I shall perhaps write later today when he returns.

Love, Mem

Later

Father is not yet back. But people are still growling and spatting here because they are all feeling so cooped up as they gaze at land. Master and Mistress Bilgewater had a real go-round on towards noon and Mam clapped her hands right over my ears so I wouldn't hear the disgusting word Mistress Billington screeched out at her husband. And then I think he called her something worse but Mam had a good fix on my ears and was pressing so hard it hurt and I couldn't hear even the first sound. If I have ear damage I am going to blame it on the Bilgewaters. They are the most vile of families.

Mam says she is worried about Dorothy Bradford as she seems quite withdrawn and she fears she is missing little John more than ever.

Love, Mem

November 12, 1620
Cape Cod Harbour

Dear Imp,

'Tis so exciting! Father returned after supper last night. They came laden with wood, the best of which is juniper for it be so fragrant. Father cut me a small branch and I plan to keep it near my head as I sleep. But there are all kinds of trees – birch, holly, pine, sassafras, walnut, oak – all without much undergrowth, making it easy to move through. He says the piece of land we gaze on from the ship is actually just a very narrow neck.

Father and the party of men did not encounter any Indians. Everyone seemed relieved but I must confess that I am slightly disappointed.

Today being the Sabbath nobody went ashore nor did work of any kind. Tomorrow, however, we all get to go ashore. The women to do washing as it will be blue Monday! Imagine washing clothes in the New World! Am I silly? I never thought washing clothes could be so exciting. I can hardly sleep waiting for blue Monday!

Imp, I am going to tuck you right under the juniper branch. Sweet sleep!

Love, Mem

November 13, 1620
On the beach, Cape Cod Bay

D<small>ear</small> Imp,

I pause for just a moment in this most wonderful morning to catch you up. We came ashore early under an armed guard organized by Captain Standish and the very first thing we did was fall to our knees on the sand to give thanks to our Lord. Then all the women began scrubbing and beating and rinsing the heaps of clothes. But we children were so wild with the thrill of the sand beneath our feet that we indeed ran wild, skirting the foam of the waves.

We flung ourselves on the wind, then raced up some nearby dunes! And not an upgrown doth scold us for I imagine that they think we need to do this. So I thank the Lord that I am a child, for although last night I felt that to do washing in the New World was the finest thing ever, first I must race one more time down this beach with Hummy and holler into the breeze.

The Billington boys found some sticks of driftwood and have been chasing the younger children around with them. The ship's carpenter took away the sticks when they chased the small ones to near where he and the men are working on the repair of the shallop. He did threaten to thrash them if he ever saw them raising sticks again in what he called a "menacing manner." The men are very hard at work on the shallop as many of its seams did open with so many people sleeping in it. The shallop is the best kind of small boat for exploring the coastline. So 'tis very important that she be quickly mended. Father helps, too. He is so good with a draw knife and fashioning new pieces.

Later

Hummy and I have now settled down to washing with the women. But we along with several other children found some tidal flats with marvellous shellfish. We plan to go gather many of these clams and mussels for all of us be ravenous for some fresh food. There are many varieties of clams.

Love, Mem

PS The only one who did not whoop and holler and run was Mary Chilton, the one we call Air Nose because she has such a high opinion of herself. She didn't help with the washing, either. Seems she is too good for work or play.

November 14, 1620
Cape Cod Harbour

Dear Imp,

Can hardly write. We all be terribly sick with the scours. 'Twas the mussels that did us in! Thankfully Father was spared, for he goes on the first big exploration trip tomorrow. Shallop still not ready, so they go on foot.

Love, Mem

PS Air Nose has lowered her nose ever so much more. Scours does that to one. 'Tis a humbling experience!

November 15, 1620
Cape Cod Harbour

Dear Imp,

Feeling slightly better. Father left quite early but Hummy and I managed to get up to see him off. We heard that the men who go on this second exploration would be bringing gifts to give the feathered men, if indeed they encounter them. It so excited me that I said to Hummy, would it not be wonderful to think of the Indians having something we made? She did agree. So, sick as we were, we managed to fashion three little poppets out of ribbon. They look quite cunning. Even the one Blessing tried to eat. The child is still so mouthy – everything goes in her mouth. We must watch her very carefully.

Father will be gone some few days on this trip and I be so impatient to hear what he has learned.

Very impatiently yours, Mem

November 16, 1620
Cape Cod Harbour

Dear Imp,

We are all stunned. We are so lucky to be alive. You can never believe what horrific thing nearly befell us. The Billington boys nearly blew up *Mayflower*! They have now been thrashed within an inch of their lives, this time by their own father. I doubt they shall ever do a bad thing again.

Here is what happened. They have been bored and cantankerous ever since we have arrived. It seems they think that they should be included on all of these exploration trips, and so were becoming increasingly unruly. Of course, none of our parents wants us to associate with these foul-mouthed, smudgy-minded little boys. So they were left to their own devices, as it were!

Poking around the ship they found some quills, the kind used for firing cannons and the like. They took these and some way broke into the ship stores and stole some gunpowder which they stuffed down into the quills. Then – the gruesome mind can indeed be a clever one – they got some rope and soaked it in saltpeter so it would light, this providing them with a slow match, and began setting the quills off with a bang. Not big bangs mind you, for the quills did not have that much gunpowder in them. They would go in a low arc with a sizzle and a pop. But guess where they were doing this – right next to kegs of gunpowder! Had one landed in the wrong place the whole *Mayflower* could have been blown sky-high! By the grace of God, it was Richard Sawyer, Hummy's father, who discovered them. And if anything good comes out of this, perhaps it is that Master Sawyer seems a bit less withdrawn and melancholy. There is more light in his eye. Perhaps nearly having one's head blown off increases one's appreciation for life.

Love, Mem

November 18, 1620
Cape Cod Harbour

Dear Imp,

Father returned at dawn this morning and what tales he has to tell! And he be so dear a man that even in this forsaken place he brings me back gifts from the New World – a small vial of fresh spring water and a painted Indian bead!

When they set out three days ago they followed along the beach for some time, then turned inland and had gone but barely a mile when they spotted their first feathered men. The men tried to follow the Indians, but the Indians quickly disappeared. The men still tried to follow their trace for another ten miles, but then night fell and they had to find lodging. By morning they were ready to resume their trek, and came upon a spring – the first freshwater they have tasted since leaving England. My father said 'twas the best he ever drank in all his life. It was from this spring that he drew a small vial for me. I have taken but a sip and I do agree. It is the best.

Now refreshed, they headed south and passed through much sassafras and oak. For Mam, Father did bring back some sassafras root and bark, which is so good for medicines for various ailments. It was shortly after this that they discovered a small path that led directly to a mysterious mound of sand. It was on this path that father found my second gift – the painted bead.

They continued on through groves of walnut trees fairly dripping with nuts and then came upon another heap of sand. They commenced digging this mound and what should they find but a great basket of most wonderful corn of all colours – some yellow, some red, and some blue. They took as much corn as they could and thanked God for the providence of bestowing upon them this corn.

Finally they returned back to our beach and shot off their muskets to signal they were here and the sailing master went in the longboat to fetch them. So now I have the bead of a genuine New World Indian and a vial of the sweetest water and I shall never ever taste another mussel in my life!

Love, Mem

Dear Imp,

Hummy and I are bored, bored, bored! We be about to scream from boredom, but don't worry, we shan't be tempted to blow up the ship. However, endless days we linger here on board. Myles Standish is very strict about women and children going ashore. He has a powerful fear of these feathered men. It is my and Hummy's personal opinion that everyone will be most disappointed if they do not attack or cause some sort of ruckus. But that is not the only reason we are kept from shore. The harbour is not an easy one for it is difficult to go to or come from shore except at high water. One must often wade and get wet, so now many suffer from colds and coughs. The men continue to work on the shallop repairs.

Love, Mem

November 22, 1620
Cape Cod Harbour

Still bored, nothing to write about.

November 23, 1620
Cape Cod Harbour

More than bored.

November 24, 1620
Cape Cod Harbour

Dear Imp,
  Can one die of boredom?
  Love, Mem

November 26, 1620
Cape Cod Harbour

Dear Imp,

Shallop is almost repaired. There is talk of the men setting off on a second exploration. I wish I were a man. I wish I were a bird. I wish I were a whale. Anything to get off this ship.

Dorothy Bradford is talking to herself. Well, not exactly to herself, rather to little John Bradford. Hummy and I hear her. If you come upon her of a sudden and she be mumbling, she looks startled and tries to cover up. But Hummy and I just this morning saw her and she did not see us. She was staring at a barrel and carrying on so animated in her conversation that you could have sworn that little John Bradford was sitting right there atop that barrel. I felt so sorry for her.

Love, Mem

November 28, 1620
Cape Cod Harbour

Dear Imp,

Thirty-four men, my father amongst them, did set off today. Some in the shallop, others in the longboat, to make a more complete exploration of some of the nearby rivers. The weather was fierce and the day laced with crosswinds, so we are not sure how far they will get. There is talk that we shall not settle here near this beach and harbour at all, for the harbour is shallow and ill suited for shipping traffic. 'Tis said that the true object of this second exploration is to find another place for our settlement.

They shall be gone for a few days, so we must be patient yet again and wait and wonder.

Love, Mem

November 30, 1620
Cape Cod Harbour

Dear Imp,

Hoorah, the men have returned earlier than expected. They did in fact make it to the mouth of one of the rivers in the shallop and explored that river and another smaller one and the surrounding valleys. Father said they went back to the place where they had originally found the corn and found even more, and beans, too, which they brought back with them. They now call this place Cornhill. Father and all the men say that this finding of corn is a sign of the special providence of God; thus showing his great mercy upon us poor souls and thus providing us with seed corn to plant next year. And they be so blessed to find it now, as soon the ground will be frozen hard and covered with snow.

Whenever the men come close, the Indians always seem to vanish before they can get even a glimpse. This is very disappointing to Hummy and me. We are so anxious for a full and complete description of a feathered man. Where exactly do they wear their feathers? We are most curious since we have heard that they are given to going around mostly naked.

The explorers, however, did discover a new kind of Indian abode, one made with boughs bent into hoops and stuck into the ground at both ends. Into this frame were woven smaller branches and the whole was covered with woven mats and strips of bark. In the houses they found a lovely assortment of baskets made from all variety of materials including crab shells. In nearby tree hollows they found stores of venison. They brought back a few of these things with them to the ship. I wish they could have brought back a whole twig house. Father did leave the ribbon poppets that Hummy and I made and it gives us deep pleasure to think of these Indians seeing these cunning little dollies.

There is now going on a great discussion as to whether we should remain here. It is getting on to winter and with weather setting in we cannot be ranging about much longer.

I'm not sure what I think, Imp. Of course, no one is asking me. I want to be able to get off this ship and sleep on shore and have a roof over my head. But mostly I want us to all have a piece of ground in the

New World we can call our own.

  Good night, dear Imp.

  Love, Mem

December 3, 1620
Cape Cod Harbour

Dear Imp,

Have not written because nothing to write. There be unending discussions as to whether a third exploration party should be set out to find another possible place for our settlement. There is talk of another great good harbour beyond the headland. With winter closing in they must come to agreement quickly.

Many colds and coughs. I worry about Mam. She looks peaked and I hear a burr in her chest when she coughs.

  Love, Mem

December 5, 1620
Cape Cod Harbour

Dear Imp,

It is decided. The men shall be leaving tomorrow to sail in a northerly direction. Weather has turned bitter and wet. I see ice on the rigging making the halyards appear like cords of glass.

Hummy and I think that Lark is sweet on John Alden. Either that or she has developed a passion for the skills of barrel repair. Whenever he goes to check the water and beer barrels she is with him.

Love, Mem

Dear Imp,

The men, including Father, left in the shallop this morning. Although proud that he be chosen once more, Mam and I were not without real fear this time as the ten men set forth in the foulest of weather. The hard rain was turning to ice as soon as it hit anything and I could see my father's coat and hat begin to shimmer like the rigging. It would not only be cold but the clothes must weigh so heavy. And with these fierce winds 'tis easy to imagine disaster striking the shallop. Any man thus iced would sink like a stone. I pray they be safe and not gone for long.

I go below and try to amuse Blessing with some of the finger games Will taught me. But I am not as clever as Will nor are my fingers so nimble.

Love, Mem

December 7, 1620
Cape Cod Harbour

Dear Imp,

The first New World baby is born here this evening. Peregrine White slipped into life just a few moments before midnight. He be a dear little thing with a thick thatch of unruly black hair, and he be our first New World baby!

Love, Mem

December 8, 1620. Midnight
Cape Cod Harbour

Dear Imp,

A terrible accident has happened. Dorothy Bradford is dead. Her body was pulled from the water shortly before midnight on December 7. She slipped

78

on the ice-glazed upper deck and went over. And what is the worst is that I perhaps could have helped her had I been more alert for I, too, was on the upper deck. You see the poor woman has been so distracted by her grief over missing her dear son that she does not pay attention, and on a ship in a winter sea like this, one must always pay heed.

I came topside because I was having a bit of the quissies and felt that the sharp cold air might help. The night was strangely beautiful. 'Tis never quite pitch-black any longer, not since the ice came and coated everything. For indeed though it is only a quarter moon and the night vapours hang with mist, the ice doth catch any light, including the whiteness of the mist. This doth turn our decks into a time of perpetual twilight. In the gloaming of the dim moon on the iced rigging I noticed something move on the seaward rail. Thinking it was a sailor at first, I paid it no heed, but then I heard a whimpering. I knew 'twas Dorothy Bradford for that is a sound I have heard her make before. She was hunched against the rail and I can now clearly see her back shake with sobs. I wondered to myself if I should go over and try to comfort her, but I hesitated for with some folks who are so grieved 'tis best that they be left alone. But just as I was wondering, perhaps I blinked, I do not know, but I heard a thud and then a second later a splash. She had slipped right under the rail! 'Tis easy to do. One must be very cautious on the icy deck. I sprang across the deck in horror and indeed I fell flat, smashing my chin. I shrieked, got up, and went to the rail to look over. I saw her skirts billow on the water. Within seconds there were sailors and others.

"Someone over the side!"

"Man overboard!"

They lowered the longboat. It took them several minutes. I do not know how long really. I quickly slipped away. I cannot stop wondering if I somehow could have stopped all this. The poor woman so distracted and all, never minding her footing. I should have gone and talked to her but I was so afraid of disturbing her. And now she will never ever again see her dear son and he shall never see his dear mother.

Love, Mem

December 10, 1620
Cape Cod Harbour

Dear Imp,

I wonder what Master Bradford will think when he returns from the third exploration. Poor man. 'Tis a sad time aboard our ship now.

My only joy be in seeing Lark with John Alden. They appear to be most gloriously separate from all the darkness, all the rancour and the petty gossip. A different climate doth swirl about them. Was it ever this way perhaps for Dorothy and William Bradford? How can things go so wrong when love is so bright?

Good night and love, Mem

December 13, 1620
Cape Cod Harbour

Dear Imp,

Good news, at last! Father and the men returned last evening and indeed they have found a new place, superior to this one. He was in such a rush to describe the trip and this new region that he could hardly get the words out fast enough. First, they set into a bay beyond the headland where they saw many of the largish cousins to the whales, called grampus fish, and thusly decided to name this place Grampus Bay. I do feel that one of the finest things about coming into this New World is that we can become namers of places and the words be most colourful and full of our own imagination.

Once there, the men divided up, some staying with the shallop, others going ashore. Amongst the shore men was my father. They followed the track of the Indians and found a great burial site, but they did no digging. As they continued they also found Indian dwellings, but no Indians. They made their camp but were wary, for they felt the presence of the Indians about even if they could not see them. Their camp was near the beach where the shallop with the other men had now put in.

On towards morning, when they were making their way down to that beach, arrows suddenly came raining down upon them! At last Myles Standish's worst fears were realized. Most of the men, though, had left their arms some yards away. So they ran with all speed to recover them. In the meantime Captain Standish held off the feathered men with his flintlock musket. Then men down at the shallop had begun firing their pieces but the others heard them calling for a firebrand to ignite the rest. So Father himself took a log from the campfire and ran with it blazing toward the beach. None of this did anything to discourage the Indians. They were, according to Father, "valiant and lusty".

No one yet had been shot or pierced by an arrow but at length one of the Indians gave a fierce cry and they all began to run away. The men followed, shouting and still shooting off their muskets. This they did to show the Indians that they were neither afraid nor discouraged. They called this site of the combat The Place of the First Encounter. I, personally, do not think this a fitting name. I would lief call it The Place of Fire and Arrows, or some such.

They all continued on in the shallop. The wind stiffened and the waters grew troublesome. But God did again deliver these men to a safe harbour on an incoming tide. There be an island under which they took shelter. And although the sea was studded with rocks all about, again Divine providence guided them to the one sandy patch in which to put down their anchor. This be Saturday, December 10.

The next day being the Sabbath they rested and the next on Monday they sounded the harbour and found it to be most excellent. Then ashore they explored and found good tillable land and many running brooklets. This place they deemed was perfect for our company. They be calling it Plimoth after that place from which we set out in England long months ago. And tomorrow we weigh anchor to go forth to our new home. And this be it, this truly be it.

Love, Mem

December 15, 1620
Cape Cod Harbour

Dear Imp,

We weighed anchor this morning but soon had turned back as we could not make the harbour because of a northwest wind and our course lies west. 'Twas like a big fist in our face. We put in again at Cape Cod Harbour. Need I say that this part of the New World is starting to look old.

We try again tomorrow.

Love, Mem

Plimoth

December 16, 1620
Plimoth Harbour

Dear Imp,

We are now fast in Plimoth Harbour after being so long in the other place that I cannot stand to write its name again. But now at the top of my entries I can write Plimoth Harbour, and this I do not think I shall ever grow tired of. For it seems fairer than the other place from all I see and hear and this truly be the site of our permanent settlement. 'Tis exciting to think that this is where I shall someday marry and have my children and their children have children and so on through the years and into the new centuries – I pray.

I am anxious to go ashore. I know I shall need much patience for t'will be a long time coming before this settlement be built, before we have a house of our own.

Patience, I must pray for patience.

Love, Mem

December 18, 1620
Plimoth Harbour

Dear Imp,

It is one minute after midnight. The Sabbath is over, so now I can write. I did pray for Patience and it did not come! In fact, I am more impatient than ever. You see, nobody could, of course, go ashore on Sabbath. So now, today, a party shall land. But first only a few sailors and men. No women and children. And to add to this frustration there is all this dispute about where they should build the settlement – near the bay, close to the good fishing, or up yonder where 'tis best for planting. Then they talk about how we must build in the most profitable place. Because of our contract with the merchants who gave us money for this trip we must raise much crop and saleable goods to send back to pay our debt.

I understand none of this. I just want to get ashore. Hummy and I want to look for plots near each other, so we might be neighbours when finally we get to build our own houses. They promise that tomorrow the women and children shall be brought ashore.

Impatiently yours, Imp, Mem

Later

Dear Imp,

I be so angry I could burst. As we were landing, I fell off the huge stepping rock into the water. More accurately I was shoved. Three guesses who? Johnny and Francis Billington, the scummy little bilge rats! But there is another culprit as well. Air Nose! I simply detest that girl.

Here is how it happened. First Mate Clark was coming for a load of us children and women and he had the longboat. But the tide had flooded in so we could not land so far up on the beach. There be this immense rock a way down, perfect for putting people ashore on. Well, me and Hummy and Mistress Air Nose were sitting in the stern of the longboat. The Billingtons were sitting in the bow. They always crowd for the bow. So shovey are they and always wanting to be the first pointing into the breeze and they hang over the gunwales dragging their hands in the water, just like Master Jones and First Mate Clark always tell them not to.

Anyhow, the wind and the currents being such, just before we reach the rock Master Clark swings the longboat stern to because he says it makes for a safer landing. So indeed it appears that Hummy and I shall be the first on the rock. We are right there, closest to it. But then Air Nose suddenly sees an opportunity. So she starts edging up. I am surprised to see her pinched little face coming up under my elbow. I think, what is she doing here? But then I see it writ on her face. History beckoned! She wanted to be the first white child to set foot at Plimoth, and this rock was the piece she could claim that would assure her that place in history for ever and a day.

Think about it. If the tide would have been right and we could have landed on the beach, well we would have all climbed out more or less at the same time. But this rock, large but small enough to only accommodate a few, changed all that. It gave a truly specific place that their stupid feet could set down on. The place could be memorialized and stupid old Mary Chilton will have her name forever linked to this chunk of rock. She'll probably have her stupid grandchildren build a stupid statue to her here.

Well, it was not quite to be because before I knew it there was Francis Billington pushing his face up beneath my elbow, too. We were half out of the boat and half on the rock. I didn't know whose foot was first on the rock. There was one moment when I saw mine and Air Nose's and a Billington boot. But I felt Air Nose's elbow in my ribs and then I felt this huge shove from behind and I went flying off the rock into the water. Not deep mind you. My skirt only half wet but when I picked myself up I saw Air Nose standing, posing really, on the rock. Master Clark had actually thrown Johnny Billington onto the beach and he had Francis by his collar, dangling him over the gunwales. And then he roared at all of us, "And they call you Christian children!" But old Air Nose just preened. I am praying very hard not to ever speak out loud the following thought, but I must say it or I shall explode. So I shall write it very very small: I hope Mary Chilton almost dies a long and painful death and then recovers but is left just slightly crippled.

Love, Mem

December 21, 1620
Plímoth Harbour

Dear Imp,

Violent storms. Wind tears through the rigging. Some pilgrims be on land with no victuals. They hope to put out the shallop later to send in provisions. We now ride on three anchors so turbulent be the seas.

Love, Mem

December 23, 1620
Plímoth Harbour

Dear Imp,

Mistress Allerton was delivered of a dead-born son last evening. They wrapped him up and put him in a small box and today we took him ashore to bury him. Winds have abated so we all go ashore today to begin some work. Men have begun felling timber. Hummy and I walked about looking for where we would most want to put our houses. Then Air Nose came along and said that her family had already picked their place and that they would probably be allowed first choice in allotment because of something to do with her father being such a distinguished tailor back in Canterbury. And then she says something about how important he and her mother were back in Canterbury, suggesting they were almost nobles. And I know this to be a bucket of pig slops because none of us on the *Mayflower* belong to those high ranks. We all be but humble, simple folk – some educated like Master Bradford and Elder Brewster, some not. So I do not know where she gets to talking in this high manner. I said to her, "Mary Chilton, if your parents get their allotment first it not be because they are so high and mighty and special. It only be because they are exactly like you – low and pushy." She screamed and ran off and Hummy turned so pale her freckles did stand out like pebbles!

Love, Mem

Dear Imp,

Yesterday when we returned to the ship, we heard of another death, a man that I hardly knew but it still seems nonetheless sad. Many of us are becoming ill. There be two sailors, one the quartermaster and the other the cook, who have also gone on. 'Tis brutal to get cold and wet as nearly all have at some point. Since this harbour be so shallow and we be more than a mile from the shore we often get drenched going in. And Father says we are not well nourished after so long without fresh food and that the illness they call scurvy is seizing upon us. So six have died this month. Mam and Father do not let me go ashore today as there is a cold wet wind and there have been cries of Indians heard. So Captain Standish has posted an extra guard. I pray, Dear Imp, that none of my family falls to this illness, nor Hummy.

Love, Mem

December 25, 1620
Plimoth Harbour

Dear Imp,

Today work begins on the Common House and a platform is built atop the hill for fortification. The cannon has already been put ashore. Captain Standish supervises that. The men cut and fell logs. Those like Father who are skilled with saws and drawknives rive and split and shape the logs. We children have been given a job, too. We walk along the shore and look for roof thatch. Though many of us be weak and tired we do this with great spirit. For the sooner the Common House is built, the sooner our own houses may be built and we shall have shelter from the winter and no more trips back and forth to the *Mayflower*.

The sailors and many of the Strangers do not understand how we can work on Christmas Day. But it is not the Sabbath so we may work. Many of the sailors would prefer to drink their beer and make merry.

Love, Mem

December 28, 1620
Plimoth Harbour

Dear Imp,

The allotments be marked out today. The ground was measured. I went along to watch them do it. They first decided how many families we actually be amongst our company, so they might calculate the number of dwellings to be built. It was decided that all single men with no families be included in the house of another. I do hope that perhaps we can have John Alden. I like him so, and then Lark would come to visit us a great deal.

Greater families were given larger plots, eight feet, or half a pole, in breadth and nearly 50 feet, or three pole in length. We do not qualify as a greater family. So our plot be the same in width but not quite so long at 45 feet. I think this is fair. I am glad they decided to chop the length rather than the breadth. A narrow house makes me feel fairly tight and bound, as if I cannot breathe.

Love, Mem

December 29, 1620
Plimoth Harbour

Dear Imp,

It is wet and cold today and brewing up to a storm. The people are sore to go to work. From the deck I can see columns of smoke rising from the Indian fires. Still I have yet to see an Indian.

Love, Mem

December 30, 1620
Plimoth Harbour

Dear Imp,

More stormy weather. Too beastly for the men to work. Mam is very tired and coughs. I play with Blessing and I think I am getting better with the finger games for I seem to engage her longer.

Love, Mem

January 1, 1621
Plímoth Harbour

So Dear Imp,

The year hath turned and I now write a new numeral on this page. But it leads me to wonder if we came at the wrong time of year for this task. Perhaps it would have been better if we had waited another year in Holland and left in the spring of 1621, so we could arrive in the summer. How shall we ever build anything here between the storms and all our people getting so sick. More have become ill. Work resumes today as there is a let-up in the weather.

Love, Mem

PS I have a most fierce craving for a warm slice of ginger cake, the kind the baker on Helmerstraat near the canal sells. This is not the first time I have thought of Holland, but it is the first time I have almost tasted it.

January 2, 1621
Plimoth Harbour

Dear Imp,

All I think of is ginger cake. I can now almost smell it, sometimes in my dreams!

The Common House proceeds well in its construction.

Love, Mem

January 3, 1621
Plimoth Harbour

Dear Imp,

I am still having my ginger dreams and now Hummy, too, is thinking about ginger cake.

We told Mam. She laughed and then she got this strange grimace while she was laughing as if it hurt but was quick to cover it up. And I was not sure whether it be a physical pain or perhaps she, too, misses Leyden and wishes we had not come, at least not now.

Love, Mem

Dear Imp,

It is reported that Captain Standish be taking some men to try and meet with any Indians that might be in the place where they had spied the fires.

Love, Mem

January 5, 1621
Plimoth Harbour

Dear Imp,

This is a very special day for me. I am taking you ashore at Plimoth for the first time. I am sitting near the construction of the Common House as I write this. Hummy and I be hoping the weather blows up and we will get to stay overnight in this little lean-to Father has fixed, which seems quite cosy. Yesterday, when Captain Standish went in search of the Indians, he shot an eagle and today for our noonday meal we had several pieces. It tastes just like mutton. Quite delicious. The sun broke out for scattered minutes through the morning. Whenever that happens I feel, maybe 'tis not so bad that we came now.

Love, Mem

Dear Imp,

I wager that you never thought you would hear me say that I admire or be envious of anything to do with a Bilgewater. But I am! For today Francis Billington has discovered a great new water beyond the highest hill. This water be divided into two great lakes. They say that the bigger of the two lakes is at least five miles around and in the middle is an island that may be close to 600 feet in length. What a fine thing to discover. Hummy and I are consumed with envy, but Mam says envy be the worst of all sins. So I am trying hard to forget about it. But it is difficult, when people are already referring to it as the Billington Sea. Oh, can you imagine a Whipple Sea with a little island in the middle called Remember?

Love, Mem

January 9, 1621
Plimoth Harbour

Dear Imp,

Weather still holds so Hummy and I take Blessing ashore. We must keep her on her lead ribbons for fear she will run off to where they are felling timber and get smacked by a falling tree. Mam is not well at all, but she does not seem to have what they call the General Sickness like the others. She coughs and she is extremely fatigued, but thank heavens no fever.

Love, Mem

January 11, 1621

Plimoth Harbour

Dear Imp,

Master Bradford, who has been staying on shore

along with Father and some of the others who work on the building, has fallen ill. He is quite sick.

Love, Mem

January 12, 1621
Plimoth Harbour

Dear Imp,

Master Bradford still quite ill. Governor Carver also has fallen ill. And now more to add to this grim news. Two young men have been lost today. They went out to gather thatch and are not back. 'Tis a miserable night, too. Lord knows how they will survive. We all pray for them.

Love, Mem

January 13, 1621
Plimoth Harbour

Dear Imp,

The two men still are lost. I think it will be a miracle
if they live.

Love, Mem

January 15, 1621
Plimoth Harbour

Dear Imp,

Two miracles in one day, and the Sabbath day at
that. Yesterday was Sunday and the first miracle is
that the lost men have returned. They are in excellent
health, but spent miserable, cold nights. The second is
that the roof of the Common House caught fire early
on the Sabbath morning from a spark that flew into

the thatch. It only burned the roof but the real miracle here was that Master Bradford and Master Carver lay sick inside with their muskets beside them. Had they not risen quickly, despite their illness, the sparks from the roof could have caught the gun powder from their muskets and they would have been blown up. But through God's mercy they and all abed in the Common House escaped.

We had our first Sabbath service on land this day also. I did so enjoy it and even though we be Saints, whose church resides in our hearts, 'twas very good at last to have firm ground under our feet for this church in our hearts.

Love, Mem

January 29, 1621
Plimoth Harbour

Dear Imp,

It has been almost two weeks since I last wrote. And today I should write with great joy as finally we are moved into our own house at last. But it is a day of sorrow. Rose Standish died in the middle of the night. I have never seen a face so carved with grief as that of Myles Standish as he held his wife in his arms when she breathed her last, and this be a man that hast been on many a battlefield and seen his comrades slew in most brutal ways. But this is his life's comrade and this small shed in which the sick now lie is his cruellest battleground, I do believe.

He sat there cradling the dear sweet woman for more than an hour after she passed on. Then John Goodman and my father carried Rose out of the shed to soon be buried.

There has of late been nothing but sickness and death. This is why I have not written. It is, however, amazing that several houses have been built and this new shed for the sick.

Mam herself has rallied some and helps when she can in the sick house, but Father and I both worry about her. She does not look well and she still coughs. But I think she is very happy to have a house now and some place of her own to sleep at night. Tomorrow … pray no more die.

Love, Mem

February 4, 1621
Plimoth Harbour

Dear Imp,

'Tis near dawn and I have taken Lark's place in the sick shed. Her own mother is now quite ill and her father as well. They have also brought in Edward Potts. His poor wife, Hannah, is large with child and she is trying to cradle his head in his feverish deliriums. It be too much for her or anyone. Hummy offered to help but she said no, she would do his nursing.

Anyhow, our house is tight and cosy. The proof was last night when the wind did damage to some of the other roofs of houses but not ours. Our house is probably the tightest in the settlement as Father is the best man with an adze and a drawknife. And it is all in the shaping of the logs that makes a tight house. He and I worked like beings possessed to get the wattle in the walls. But I do believe this to be my speciality. 'Tis surprising because I am not so good with stitchery, and with wattle one must weave small twigs in between the studs and framing, something like

110

stitchery. Then over that we put the plaster mixed from sand, clay, water and grass. We have all but one wall plastered now.

What with so many getting sick it hath taken me away from the work. But Blessing is actually quite good at helping Father with the mixing of the plaster and he has given her some small places to squash it into. And she does not try to eat it! That be the amazing part. Remember how I told you she be so mouthy? She thinks this plastering is playing. She loves doing it. The Lord does work in mysterious and beautiful ways and I think one of them is through Blessing – that she can think that building this house is a game and do it well is wondrous. It keeps her busy and gives Mam a rest.

We have of course no chairs, no beds, just pallets, no tables – but tomorrow Father says he shall put up some pegs so we might hang our clothes. The fireplace is good and draws well and the chimney does not leak. We have one kettle and some pots we brought with us as well as a lug pole from which to hang the pots and such. Father has not had time to fix them into the fireplace yet. Although we do have a spit in place. Now if we could only get some meat to roast on it. But game has been scarce. We do have our one window in place in the west wall. Mam will not permit one in the south wall as she believes the vapours be poor coming from the south and that they cause illness.

I am so glad Mam brought the large bolts of linen, for we have soaked them in linseed oil and put them in one square window that Father cut. It brings in a little light on the brighter days. Father plans that there be an outdoor cooking oven, too, for summer and there is space for a garden. But the notion of summer and gardens seems as far off as the moon. Oh, I must go, dear Imp, Mistress Mullins is beginning to thrash and when she does that a coughing fit is soon coming.

Love, Mem

February 5, 1621
Plimoth Harbour

Dear Imp,

Mistress Mullins now be coughing blood. Master Potts is worse and still his wife refuses to take a rest. I have not the heart to write more now.

Love, Mem

February 8, 1621
Plimoth Harbour

Dear Imp,

Master William White now joins the sick in the shed as do Mary Allerton, mother of the dead-born son, and Elizabeth Winslow, wife of Edward Winslow. I spend most of my time, however, with the More children, the little orphans from London who came as servants to the Winslows and the Carvers and Brewsters. One has already died and I fear another might follow shortly. They do not call ever for their mother but only for one and another. John keeps calling for Jasper and I have not the heart to tell him that Jasper has gone on to the Lord.

Love, Mem

113

February 9, 1621
Plimoth Harbour

Dear Imp,

We had a near terrible disaster today. The roof of the sick shed caught fire. I was terrified. At the time I was sitting by little Ellen More trying my best to engage her attention with a finger game, my heart quickening every time her swollen eyes opened and she gave a little smile. Then suddenly without warning the flames burst out with a blast of heat. I picked her right up, bedclothes and all, and ran. You know she hardly weighed a thing. Then Mistress Potts tried to pick up her husband all by herself and run. Would you believe she nearly did it? But luckily, Elder Brewster came and John Goodman.

God was merciful, however, and there was no serious damage done to the shed and soon Ellen was tucked back in. She now be calling for Jasper. What am I to do? These poor little orphans.

The best news today is that five geese were killed and distributed amongst us. So our spit turns something for the first time since we be here. I write by the light of the fire this evening and smell the dripping fat. We place a pipkin below the bird to catch it; for the fat be so good in stews and pottages and if we ever do grow anything in our garden it is good for frying up vegetables. But as I say the garden and summer seem so far off as not to be true and ever coming. I should not think this way. I am so blessed compared to those poor orphan children. If I think a garden and an outdoor oven be far off that is nothing compared to a mother and a father in heaven.

Love, Mem

February 15, 1621
Plimoth Settlement

Dear Imp,

It has been over a month since we have been living continuously on the land, and I realize that all these days I be putting the word "Harbour" at the top each time right under the date. I think it is time to call us a settlement. Perhaps it is wishful thinking as so many of us are sick and moving on to that next world. The houses of our settlement are built in two facing rows and we are more than half way up toward the fort on what they are calling the pasture land. The other side be where the crops will be planted.

There is a meeting tomorrow called for by Captain Standish. The purpose of the meeting is to organize a militia. For, in fact, today, a party of twelve Indians were seen nearby. I still have yet to see any feathered man. I hope they do not shoot them all before I get my chance. I pray to God that the Indians be good and do nothing intemperate to provoke Captain Standish.

Love, Mem

February 16, 1621
Plimoth Settlement

Dear Imp,

Strange and mysterious is the passage of some into the arms of death. Death, however, is becoming

116

ordinary around here and has found yet a new way to disturb and transfix us with its power. Early this morning as I was working in the shed it became clear that soon Edward Potts would depart this earth. His wife, who had cradled him in her arms these long last days, lay herself down right beside him on the pallet.

When he died, she continued to lie beside him for some time. We let her be. But imagine our surprise when we begin to notice that Mistress Potts was in the midst of labour! But she had hardly moaned. 'Tis very difficult to write what happened next. The women did wrap up the baby and give it to Mistress Potts, who looked upon it and a smile broke over her face like sunshine scattering across clouds. She then held the baby to her breast and showed its sweet visage to her dead husband.

It was an eerie configuration, but still we gathered round, just as if Edward Potts were alive. And for the moment we were all as happy as could be in these peculiar circumstances because for one blessed hour it seemed as if death had been defied. But then suddenly the baby seemed to grow weak and within minutes it, too, had joined its father.

They gave Hannah a very strong sleeping draught, for they were fearful that they would not be able to take her dead child and her dead husband away from her. Now she will wake up and she might think that she has merely dreamed a horrible dream. I don't know, but it does not seem like a good way to finish the business of Hannah Potts and her husband and baby son. 'Tis a very terrible thing when people try to make real parts of your life unreal.

Love, Mem

February 17, 1621
Plimoth Settlement

Dear Imp,

Mam has indeed fallen ill. They have brought her to the sick shed. I resisted for several days, hoping against hope that she had not indeed sunk to the terrible level of those in the sick shed. But Father and I realized last night that we only be fooling ourselves. 'Tis better she move to the sick shed where me and Hummy and Lark and the other dear people who care for them are. And most important I can always be there for her now. Blessing can go with Mistress Brewster and her lot. She seems happy enough there. Love and Wrestling are quite good with her. Oh Imp, I'm so frightened I can barely think. But I just pray and try not think. Pray for my dear Mam.

Love, Mem

February 18, 1621
Plimoth Settlement

Dear Imp,

Little Ellen More, one of the orphans from the More family, died this morning. All night long Hummy and I held her hand and all night long she called for her brothers, who both lay sick. But John did seem stronger, so Hummy and I did move his pallet closer to his sister. Then just before dawn, her breathing came easier and she opened her eyes and she looked right over at John and what did she say – "Mother!" And then she died. 'Tis very mysterious to me, but Hummy does believe that she was already at the Gates of

Heaven and did, indeed, see her long-dead mother there.

After someone dies, if there be a chance, Hummy and I usually walk outside a bit. We walk to the edge of the woods and we hardly talk at all. I'm not sure what my thoughts are. But after all the gasping and the coughing of the sick and the dying in the shed there is an astonishing silence at the woods' edge. I just empty my mind and think about the designs of the ice-sheathed branches against the sky. Sometimes, after a freezing rain, the branches catch the sun in such a way that they flare against the sky like a silver embroidery. I can only try and think of these things – there is so much blood and bile and the dark noisy gurgling of death in the shed.

Love, Mem

February 25, 1621
Plimoth Settlement

Dear Imp,

Over the past week fourteen people have died. Poor Lark now has lost everyone in her family. Thank God she has John Alden always by her side.

I have come out to the edge of the woods with you, Imp, to be away from it all. You see, I know too much of death for a child, for anyone who be not a doctor or a soldier. I know the sag of the mouth in the last hours. I know the peculiar manner in which the fingers do pick at the sheets. Why do they do that, Imp? So many of them do this odd picking. Is it that they are trying to pluck a bit of earth to take with them to the next kingdom?

Love, Mem

March 3, 1621
Plimoth Settlement

Dear Imp,

There is a teasing of spring in the air. I hate it. Seventeen people died last month and the birds are chirping. We are mocked. I want the birds to shut their beaks. I want the sun to blink once and then roll its bright yellow eye into the skull of the sky like the dead man's eyes do roll up. I want the soft, warm breeze to sputter out. I dare a dandelion to show its face!

Love, Mem

March 7, 1621
Plimoth Settlement

Dear Imp,

The weather turns cold again. The wind is from the full east. But I have some hope. Father and I decided to move Mam back to our house. The very thought of returning to it seems to have helped her. Father will take my place in the sick shed and I will stay with Mam and Blessing. Also, today we have planted seed for the first time. We sowed some in our garden as did other people. There is something that I have not mentioned before, Imp. For a long time on my saunterings to the rim of the woods, to break from the illness and death of the sick shed, I have felt when I sit there that eyes are watching from the shadowed edges of the woods. I said nothing to Hummy about it until today, but she, too, agrees. We both think that the Indians be much closer and more constant in their vigil of us then anyone has previously thought.

Love, Mem

March 9, 1621
Plimoth Settlement

Dear Imp,

Mam is back. It is so good. She still is terribly weak, but she seems most happy to be back. When she has the strength and the breath she keeps telling me all sorts of housewifery things. It is as if she wants to teach me all at once. I must grow rosemary in the garden and then put it around the house to clear the bad vapours. Also, I should grow thyme and if Blessing has nightmares give her an infusion of it.

This talk disturbs me. I say, "Why me? You shall be well, by spring. We shall plant together." And then she laughs and says that she really means for when I grow up and have a household of my own. And that I must learn how to feel the weight of a measure in my hand for many a good housewife has been cheated thus by a shopkeeper. And I say, "Mam, we barely have houses here, let alone shops. And she laughed at this and then began to cough. I must mind my tongue. But 'tis so good to have her back.

Love, Mem

124

March 10, 1621
Plimoth Settlement

Dear Imp,

Hummy is most worried about her father. It is hard to describe for it be not exactly a bodily sickness, but Master Sawyer has become increasingly slow in his movements and response. He seems withdrawn into another world. Hummy did confess to me when we were by the woods' edge that she has heard him late at night talking to her dear dead mother. It reminds her so of Dorothy Bradford. He has ceased to go with the men to fell timber and he stays much of the day staring into his fireplace. He does help with the sick though. So at least he is doing that share.

Love, Mem

March 11, 1621
Plimoth Settlement

Dear Imp,

Hummy arrived most upset today. She said her father was working in the sick shed and was tending Mistress Winslow, who appears close to death. She heard him bend over and whisper something about his wife in Mistress Winslow's ear. Then he began speaking a bit louder and she heard him very clearly say. "Tell dear Elinor that I shan't be long coming. That all shall be well." Poor Hummy! Does he not ever think of her? What shall happen to Hummy?

Love, Mem

126

March 12, 1621
Plimoth Settlement

Dear Imp,

Hummy is so embarrassed. They have asked her father not to work in the sick shed any more. He is too much of a disturbance to them that are about to die and to their poor relatives as well. No one amongst the near dying is spared the chance to be a messenger for him to his beloved Elinor. It is most eerie and disconcerting. He was whispering into the ear of a dying child, and the child in her fever said, "But how shall I know her?" And then he said something. And the child said, "But I might get lost." And the little one began to cry for fear of being lost in heaven. It is so terrible to even think about.

They have sent him with Peter Brown to hunt for thatch for the roofs. He is too distracted, Father says, to handle an axe. He might hurt himself.

I feel so awful for Hummy. I think her father is a very selfish man.

Love, Mem

March 13, 1621
Plimoth Settlement

Dear Imp,

The sailors be talking a great deal now about returning to England. They hope to leave some time in April. Of course, the holds will be empty. So the merchants who gave the money might not be pleased. But almost half our company has died and how could we do much more than keep ourselves alive? Father says that real efforts this spring and summer shall be made to begin some sort of trade in furs with the Indians and also fishing. He thinks that dried fish will even the balance sheets with the merchants, for it is very marketable. Again, I know nothing of these business affairs. Staying alive seems to be our major endeavour. It is unimaginable that somewhere in all this there could be what Father calls a "profit" – at least one that can be calculated in terms of money.

Love, Mem

March 16, 1621
Plimoth Settlement

D<small>ear</small> Imp,

Oh joy! At last I have seen an Indian. I have not only seen him I have stood right beside him. I have touched his hand. I have filled my eyes with the amber gold of his skin!

'Twas this morning, and seeing as it was warm I had opened our door a crack while I did wrestle with the cooking pots and fix Mam a mug of tea. It was only the corner of my eye that did catch this sight. And when one thinks about it 'twas all the more miraculous because the door was only opened a small slice; so 'twas as if I did glimpse a sliver of that slice but such was the strangeness of this view that it did arrest me. For that sliver was like a colourful smear of the brightest paints. There was the amber gold, then a bold streak of black and white, and somewhere a bright red mark that all came together into something like a human configuration.

I raced to the door, and there walking straight up our

129

narrow street between the two rows of our houses was a feathered man bold as anything. He be tall and straight and almost naked, save for a little scrap of leather about his waist with a bit of fringe no more than ten inches in width. Just enough to cover him. I blush as I write this. He carried a sheath with some arrows, and across his shoulder was the pelt of a dark orange fox. His hair was long at the back and twisted into a knot with a braid hanging down his neck. But in the front the hair had been shaved closely to show his whole forehead and a good part of the dome of his head. There were at least two feathers tucked into the braid!

I was so excited that I raced out of the house with Mam's mug of tea still in my hand. Everyone was pouring out of the seven houses that now line the street and he strode boldly on. Masters Bradford and Brewster and Governor Carver intercepted him. By this time I was standing very close to the Indian. And now the most startling thing of all. This feathered man opens his mouth and what comes out, but English. And here is what he said exactly: "Welcome. My name is Samoset. I come not from here, but from Monhegan to the north, by sail with a strong wind a day, by land five."

I have never seen men more stunned in my life than Elder Brewster, Master Bradford, and Governor Carver.

Samoset asked for beer and biscuits, but they gave him strong water instead and little Wrestling Brewster was sent to fetch the liquor bottle. Samoset was then taken to the Common House as others fetched the biscuits and I made it my business to fetch him something more. So I brought him a good hefty slab of pudding that I had just turned out, and Hummy getting the same idea brought a slice of mallard they had not yet eaten, and Love brought some cheese. Had it been left to the upgrowns he would have only eaten hardtack and whisky.

I do not think that the upgrowns were on purpose unfriendly, but they did appear fearful whereas we children were more fascinated than fearful and wanted to do anything to make Samoset stay and like us.

He loved all the food we brought him. The men then began to question him. Samoset told them that the region where we be is called Patuxet, which means Little Bay or Little Falls. Four years ago there was a great and terrible plague here killing every single person. Therefore there is no one now to lay claim to the land, but it is why we find many of the fields cleared. Samoset has been in this place eight months. He learned his English from Englishmen who came to fish in the waters off Monhegan. In Monhegan he was a sagamore, or a lord of his tribe. His tribe be called the Wabdnaki, or the People of the Dawn. He knew well the entire region here on Cape Cod and all the provinces and the various tribes and their leaders.

The people who we are nearest to are called the Wampanoag, which means People of the Breaking Day. But there also are the Narragansett and others. He says that the biggest chief of this region, the sachem as they call him here, is Ousamequin, or Yellow Feather. He also be called Massasoit.

Samoset talked a long time and when he was finished he showed no sign of leaving. He could have stayed for ever as far as I was concerned. He is in fact spending the night at Stephen Hopkins' house. And I heard Governor Carver whisper as they walked out, to "watch him," as if he might steal something. I felt this was not quite proper in attitude.

So good night and love,
Remember Patience Whipple

 D ear Imp,

I do not think I shall ever be bored or find life dull and tedious again – as long as the Indians keep coming. On Samoset's second visit he brought five other men with him. These wore leggings and were generally more covered. They also carried with them little pouches filled with powder. I saw Captain Standish start as he saw one pour some into his hand, undoubtedly thinking it was for a musket.

But he then took some water from a bowl which we had set before them with other victuals and rolled the powder into a paste and began eating it. Samoset explained that it was corn powder.

I walked right beside Samoset. When he was leaving, he smiled at me and said he liked the pudding I had first brought him. So I quick as could ran back and got him the last bit we had. He thanked me. That be a few days ago.

Now today he comes again and in accompaniment is

an Indian called Squanto, who also speaks English. I know this right away for, as soon as Samoset sees me he turns to Squanto and says in English, "That is the pudding girl!" So now I have a new name – The Pudding Girl. I like it. And I did make some more. This pudding is an odd one for it has none of the normal things because there be none of those normal things here, like milk and eggs and butter. I make it with fat from the geese drippings or whatever fowl we can get, dried peas soaked in beer, and some of the flour we brought from Leyden, and the dried currants and the dried fruits of which we still have a goodly supply.

Squanto and Samoset talked with us for maybe an hour and then they mentioned that the great sachem Massasoit and his brother be nearby, in fact, just behind the ridge with 60 or more of his people. Captain Standish jumped up quite alarmed. But Samoset said there was no need for that, they came to parley. So Captain Standish and the Governor met Massasoit and his brother. A treaty was worked out. This treaty is one of peace and we pledge that we shall not injure each others' people, nor steal from them, and if there be an unjustly war against the Indians we shall help them.

Good night and Peace!

Love, Mem – or "The Pudding Girl"

PS I gave Squanto some of the pudding. I pray that he likes it as much as Samoset.

March 25, 1621
Plimoth Settlement

Dear Imp,

Hummy's father has not come out of their house for two days! Hummy is worried to death. She knows not what to do with the man. And I am no help.

If Hummy's father has not come out, Mistress Billington certainly has – and at odd times. She be abroad two nights in a row now, "up to no good," says people. Why would someone go out at night in the vapours especially when a south wind is blowing? There is talk that she keeps a sieve and scissors for the practice of what is called the small sorceries – fortune-telling and the like. Lark says she knows not about such things. She only does know that Mistress and

Master Billington fight loudly all the time, for she lives closer to them. And that one day Governor Carver reprimanded Master Billington for talking so coarsely to his wife outdoors where everyone can hear. I myself do not think it matters – outdoors, indoors, upside down, or right side up – it is still poor to talk that way to any woman.

Love, Mem

March 27, 1621
Plimoth Settlement

Dear Imp,

More excitement. Samoset brought to our house some dried pumpkin, which he showed us how to string along with some Indian corn. We hang it up in the rafters and it makes for a colourful decoration. Mam loves it and, as she is feeling weak, has spent much time on her pallet looking up at the bright orange and yellow. She says it is like a garden growing in the ceiling.

Hummy's father seems much improved. In fact, he looked at Hummy yesterday when I was there and smiled as if he had seen her for the first time in months. This makes Hummy's and my hearts both swell.

Father has returned this afternoon from treading for eels with Samoset. They caught so many – big fat ones that we shall make into a stew.

Love, Mem

April 1, 1621
Plimoth Settlement

Dear Imp,

The month hath turned and, although it be rainy, Squanto says it is the beginning of the time for corn planting. He calls these days *Seequanakee'wush*. I cannot believe it but perhaps spring and gardens are truly coming.

Squanto promises we shall see the corn shoots by June! We spend the whole day planting corn. The rain stops and the sun comes out and I start to laugh, for

Hummy has not minded her hat and her face has grown so many freckles. I say I hope we have as much corn as she has freckles on her face.

Love, Mem

April 2, 1621
Plimoth Settlement

Dear Imp,

'Tis the worst imaginable. When I return home I find Blessing crying uncontrollably and Mam coughing blood. Oh Imp, I am so ashamed. All these days I have been so taken with the Indians I have neglected my own dear mam. I mean not neglected her in duty. I have helped her and brought her tea and carried her to the privy, but I have been blind. So full have my eyes been with the colour and the feathers of the Indians that I have not seen my mother fade before me. I should have known that she was growing weaker.

She be so weak now she can hardly talk. She does look at the pumpkins we have strung on the ceiling and the corn. I explained to Samoset and Squanto how she loves that colour and the dear souls bring more for me to string, along with some golden tansy that is dried. Father puts it up. Mam watches. It is silly, I know, but I have this notion that if she keeps watching the yellow she loves that floats above her head, that somehow this will stay death. That she will not need to go to heaven. That is if we can string these yellow beauties just so…

I can write no more. I am too fearful.

Love, Mem

April 3, 1621
Plimoth Settlement

Dear Imp,

Mam died this morning. She died with her eyes locked on the yellow of the pumpkins and the tansy. She died with two words on her parched lips: "I love." There was not time for the rest but we knew her meaning all the same. I be feeling so strange. I have no

139

mother now. I have no mother. I keep repeating that to myself. But I cannot believe she is gone.

Love, Mem

April 4, 1621
Plimoth Settlement

Dear Imp,

I have yet a new grief. Hummy sails tomorrow with her father on the *Mayflower*. That is when the ship is to leave. He must go back to England to be near the grave of his dear Elinor, he says. I am simply numb.

This morning we buried Mam. Father made the coffin last night. We wrapped her in a wool shroud and I put in thyme to ward off nightmares and rosemary for remembrance. We had brought these herbs from Leyden. And, of course, I put in the brightest of the tansy.

Love, Mem

April 5, 1621
Plimoth Settlement

Dear Imp,

I watched from the hillock until the *Mayflower* was but a speck on the horizon. Hummy and I decided not to say goodbye on the beach in front of the others, but early in the morning by the rim of the forest. She cried, but it is as if I still be too numb. She promises to come back some day – even if it must be as an indentured servant. She tried to give me every hope. She even said that if her father soon died, she would offer her service to another family for there is supposedly another ship coming next autumn. So we hugged by the edge of the forest and that was it. I watched the rest from here where I now still sit with you, Imp, my sole companion.

Oh Imp, I have lost so much. And to think a few short days ago I dared believe in spring again, but I was right the first time. It shall always be a winter in my head. I am black in my heart and full of wrath. I shall write no more for a long time.

Love and goodbye, Mem

June 5, 1621
Plimoth Settlement

Dear Imp,

It has been a long time, has it not? How be you? Do you remember me? I must write these odd, short sentences. The words creak rusty in my head. My fingers are stiff. The pen lays heavy in my hand. I will try tomorrow.

Love, Mem

June 6, 1621
Plimoth Settlement

Dear Imp,

Here I be again. I live, Imp, that is all. I concentrate very hard on small things. I get up in the morning. I put on my stockings, my garters, my three petticoats, my waistcoat – an old moss-green one of Mam's, my apron, my pocket I tie round my waist, my coif, my shoes. I now have pegs for all these things. Father made them for me. I am not sure when. I have lost track of time.

My fingers feel less stiff. Perhaps I shall write more tomorrow.

Love, Mem

June 7, 1621
Plimoth Settlement

Dear Imp,

This is who has died since I last wrote in April. John Carver and then a few days later his wife. But the dying from the General Sickness has slowed. William Bradford is now our governor. It strikes me as very odd that the Billingtons are the one family that has remained untouched by the General Sickness. Every other family that is here has lost someone.

There has been one marriage, Edward Winslow and

Susannah White, both of whom lost their mates in the sickness.

I can write no more today.

Love, Mem

June 15, 1621
Plimoth Settlement

D_{ear} Imp,

You shall never believe what young John Billington has gone and done now. He went and got himself lost for nearly five days. The bothersome child had everyone running all over creation. Governor Bradford called a meeting with Massasoit, who sent out the word. Then word did come a day later. The horrid child had found his way to the Nauset Indians, the very same people who had set upon our men with their bows and arrows in December. But did they set upon John Billington? No. They adored the child! Governor Bradford sent the shallop for him yesterday. He returned today triumphant, bedecked in feathers and beads, more wampum then you could shake a stick at. These Billingtons have more lives than a dozen cats. Not that I wish him dead, but how come he got to go to an Indian village, stay five days and get presents, and not me? It sticks in my craw, it does!

Love, Mem

PS Imp, my hand feels ever so much looser now. The words no longer rusty.

June 17, 1621
Plimoth Settlement

Dear Imp,

Did I tell you that Squanto has embraced our faith and has become a professed Member of the Holy Discipline? He be a Saint now like so many of us. But even before, there never was any doubt that Squanto was, as Master Bradford hath said so many times, "a special instrument sent of God" for all of our good and beyond our greatest expectation. For indeed the corn begins to blaze in the field and we shall not face starvation next winter.

Love, Mem

June 30, 1621
Plimoth Settlement

Dear Imp,

We be busy sunrise to sunset now. The one strip of rye seeds that were planted in the spring has done well and many of us girls and women are out there binding it into sheaves. 'Tis a quick-growing seed, the rye. Then our own gardens need constant tending. All this is hot, sweaty work and the mosquitoes are fierce. There is very little time to write. Father promises me that I can go with him and Squanto and Hobomok and see how they tread for eels. I am most anxious to do this. I forgot to tell you. Hobomok is another Indian, a friend of Squanto who now has become a part of our small village. He, too, likes my pudding.

There is beginning to be talk of a major exploration to the province known as Massachusetts, where there is a great bay. The Indians there are said to have many furs. This is important for we soon must have things to send back to England for the merchants who await payment on their investment. Their ship will be

146

coming in the autumn. I forbid myself to think of Hummy and the possibility she might be on it. But it is very hard. Especially when I think of certain things, such as how much Hummy would love to go and tread for eels. But I must not think of this, nor of Mam, either, whom Blessing begins to resemble more and more every day.

Love, Mem

July 5, 1621
Plimoth Settlement

Dear Imp,

We had to wait until the moon was full to go eeling, and then Father and I had to arrange for Mistress Hannah Potts to come over and stay with Blessing. We go with Squanto to the great pond that connects with the sea. There be a place between the pond and the sea where the water narrows into a river. Squanto has brought two eel traps.

Father tells me I must stand in the bushy reeds that

grow at the edge and not get my feet wet. "Why, Master Whipple?" Squanto asks. "Mistress Pudding would be good at wading and beating the water." But Father explains that it be not proper for young girls to bare their ankles and wet their skirts in such a manner. He gives me a long branch, however, so I can reach over and beat from the banks.

Father wades up toward the pond and beats while Squanto stands with the trap and waits. The moonlight being so bright, I can see clearly as if it were daylight and soon notice the stirring in the water and even the darkish shapes. I am in charge of getting them into the basket as Squanto and my father bring them up from the trapping. They slither and flop and catch the moonlight on their glistening dark skins. Some we shall turn into eel pie, a favourite of ours. A portion, however, will be salted and dried and put in the keg to go back to England for the merchants to sell.

Love, Mem

July 26, 1621
Plimoth Settlement

Dear Imp,

For some time now, though I did not want to say anything for sure, I think that there be an attraction between my father and Mistress Potts. I am not sure how I feel about it quite honestly. On one hand, I would be most terribly disturbed if Father became like Hummy's father, trying to speak to Mam through folks who be half dead and be more interested in heaven than what he has here on earth – namely me and Blessing and this house that is so tight and our garden, which is doing well. Yet, on the other hand it seems soon after Mam's death. I do realize, however, that Edward Winslow remarried barely a month after his wife passed on.

Still. I don't know. I mean Mistress Potts seems nice enough, but she is strange. Of course, it is understandable after all she has been through.

She is so quiet. That is the hardest. She hardly ever says a word. I have worked with her planting in the fields, right next to her, and she never speaks. If she feels I am doing something wrong, she never objects directly to the way I do it, never says it out loud, but she will just go and do it over again. I almost rather have her say, "That is not right." She is very placid, too. Never smiles. I'm just not sure if she would really fit in here with us. It's not as if we are raucous, but she has this stillness about her that goes beyond reason. Perhaps with Father she is not so still. I cannot imagine how he could be drawn to her.

Love, Mem

August 1, 1621
Plimoth Settlement

Dear Imp,

Father has made me a stool! – a stool, Imp, just for me. I think I might be the only child in the settlement to have a stool all to her own. And it be the first piece of real furniture in our house. We have not bed nor table. We just use a barrel for a table. I do not count shelves or pegs as furniture. It was so dear of him. He is making a real spoon for Blessing. There hardly are any spoons or forks in the entire settlement. I do not know when he found the time for this work. We are so busy from before dawn till darkness what with tending the garden and fields and at least every other day he goes fishing, and when we are not doing one of those chores we are making nets for the fishermen. I have never worked so hard before. This is why I can only get to writing you every few days or so. And it will get worse as the time of harvest nears. Already I can feel the light being sliced off the day's end, just a tiny sliver at a time.

But think of it, Imp. I have my stool and shall sit by the fire on it for a winter's eve. If only Mam were here, how cosy it would be. I wonder if one ever grows old enough not to miss her mother?

Love, Mem

August 2, 1621
Plimoth Settlement

Dear Imp,

Guess who else has a stool?

Air Nose!

Love, Mem

August 5, 1621
Plimoth Settlement

Dear Imp,

Here is something else I do not like about Mistress Hannah Potts. She "tsks" when she doesn't like something or the manner in which something is being done. I was working with her in the pea patch today and I heard this tsk-tsking sound. At first I thought it to be a gigantic, annoying mosquito, but no, it was

152

Hannah Potts. Sticking her little tongue between her lips tsking at the way I was snapping off the pea pods. She then tsked very loudly and said, "Like this." That was all, a tsk and two words. I don't like that. It is very irritating.

Love, Mem

August 9, 1621
Plimoth Settlement

Dear Imp,

I feel simply terrible. I hope Mam in heaven was not looking on, but undoubtedly she was. After four days in the pea patch with Hannah Potts and her tsking, I turned to her and I said, "Can't you just say what I am doing wrong? Tell me, instead of this tsking and clicking with your tongue?" Well, her face did crumple right before me. Her lovely grey eyes swam with tears, and she fled the field. And if I didn't feel bad enough then, I find here when I return a note folded on my pallet.

Here it is:

Dear Remember,

I am so sorry to have talked as you have described. It is not good of me and this might be very hard for you to understand, but since my dear husband died and my baby, too, is now buried at his side, I have had a very hard time speaking. I cannot always put my thoughts into words. I am getting better but speech comes very hard for me. My tsk sounds do not really always denote criticism. With the peas it is nothing that you are doing wrong but the fact that so many of them seemed scorched. Our yield be so small for all the work we have done. But I cannot think how to express it. I know you are a patient child and will now understand better my affliction.

May God's blessings be upon you,
Hannah Potts

She knows I am a *patient* child, Imp. Oh dear, I be mortified. The poor thing.

Love, Mem

August 15, 1621
Plimoth Settlement

Dear Imp,

I went out today to a field near the pond where Father and Squanto and I had gone eeling. I picked a lovely bunch of wild flowers. They be New World wild flowers so I know not the name. But they make a lovely bouquet. As I stared down at them, I thought this would be a nice thing to do for Mistress Potts. So I stuck them in our smallest pipkin with water and left them at her house with a note. For over a week now I have been trying to think of a way to make up for my rudeness. I know this cannot make up really, but perhaps it shows a better aspect of me.

Love, Mem

August 20, 1621
Plimoth Settlement

Dear Imp,

There is more talk these last days about the expedition to the Massachusetts province. Father is to be included. Everyone is very excited. The only problem is that it will leave us short-handed at a very busy time of the year – harvest. This is when I wish more than ever that I be a boy and could go with them.

Love, Mem

August 25, 1621
Plimoth Settlement

Dear Imp,

Today I was out in the field near the large pond. I wandered to the inland end of the pond and heard children laughing. It could have been our pilgrim children, for when Indian children laugh it does sound just like ourselves, which makes me think all children on earth must laugh alike. I crept closer and crouched down in the berry bushes and peered through. There, where the lily pads grow so thick, a half a dozen Indian children were swimming and diving. When they came up they clutched the roots of water lilies. They are gathering them for something. I shall ask Squanto.

But what is amazing to me is that these children are so strong and healthy despite playing about in the water. We have been taught to fear water, not simply because one might drown but because we think that it washes off the body's natural protection. I am beginning to wonder about this now. I think if it is not true, I should like to learn how to swim. I, of course, would not go naked. Fear not, Imp. I would wear at least two petticoats, my waistcoat and my coif. I would not wear shoes, but yes, stockings.

Love, Mem

August 26, 1621
Plimoth Settlement

Dear Imp,

I asked Squanto about the water lily roots. He says that they are dried and pounded into a powder that heals stiffness of joints as well as stomachaches!

I want to go back there. I am haunted by it. I have figured out a better swimming dress. I would wear my two petticoats and my blouse, but not the waistcoat. I would then tie the third petticoat under my arms, smock-style, which will be as modest as the waistcoat but allow more movement.

Love, Mem

September 1, 1621
Plimoth Settlement

Dear Imp,

We have been so busy gutting, salting and packing fish in barrels that I have not had time to get back to the water lily place until yesterday and there was no one there. I was most bitterly disappointed. But then in walking closer to the pond's edge I found a narrow but well-worn path. So I began to follow it and came upon a very small cluster of wigwams. This must be the one settlement that Squanto had told Father and me about on the night we went eeling. He had said that this was a good summer camp, for the people were near where the eels swam and not too far to dig the clams on the beach and gather the crabs.

There was good clay here, too, for there be a small creek or river that runs nearby. I have never seen so closely the wigwam houses of the Indians. They are like lovely wooden bowls turned upside down with coverings of bark. They have racks with strings of drying quahogs and other fish. I saw one woman shaping a pot of clay. I want to go back again. How I wish Hummy were here. Once we felt the eyes at the rim of the forest peering at us, but now I am the eyes and I am looking at them. And it be such a different world I do see.

Love, Mem

September 4, 1621
Plimoth Settlement

Dear Imp,

I went again today. This time I was able to follow two women to the river bed. There were more Indians there digging clay, and the children were splashing and swimming in the cloudy water. I am becoming convinced that water cannot hurt one that much. I must figure out a way to learn how to swim.

Love, Mem

September 6, 1621
Plimoth Settlement

D_{ear} Imp,

The most astounding thing happened today. Once more I went to the water lily place and followed the narrow path and then crouched in the bushes to watch the activity in the summer camp. And guess what, Imp? I was discovered. By Squanto no less. I felt so embarrassed to be found peeping in like that. I didn't know what to say. So I just blurted out how curious I was and how unfair it seemed to me that only the men ever got to go and meet with the Indians. And just like that Squanto said, "Come with me."

He took me right into the camp and introduced me to the Indians. I think the children were just as curious about me as I was about them, for they did gather around me and touch my skirts and apron. Their mothers tried to reprimand them, for this was considered too forward, I guess. But I smiled and I took off my apron. I handed it to one little girl so she could see it. Another pointed to my coif... Well, Imp,

161

I know, 'tis unbelievable, but I took it off and let her try it on. Everybody did gasp when they saw my hair. It had turned so bright since I had been careless about wearing my cap. They brought me right into one of their wigwams. It was the loveliest time.

I was in this dome of shadows with the sweet fragrance of bark and mosses and 'twas almost as if I were living in the heart of a tree and there be in this particular wigwam a newborn Indian baby, no more than a few days old, and he be swaddled so carefully in doe skin and then bound to what Squanto told me is a papoose board. They can prop him up anywhere or carry him on their backs. And they gave me some mashed corn in a hollowed-out bowl that had some berries in it.

And I did learn so much. I learned that, because they have already heard the locusts singing, the time of the frost be near. I learned that they call the insects Little People, which I find most dear. I learned that these months, August and September, which they call moons, are called *Neepunnakee'wush*, which means the time when the corn can be eaten. I have learned so many new words. But this day was indeed my happiest day ever in the New World. In some ways I feel it to be my first day here.

Love, Mem

September 16, 1621
Plimoth Settlement

Dear Imp,

The men prepare to go on the expedition to the north where the Massachusetts Indians live, and Father prepares to go with them. Tonight Father came to me. I think I knew what he was going to say before he said it. He asked how I would like to have Hannah Potts be my stepmother and his wife. I simply did not know what to answer, my feelings being so stirred up. Finally I blurted out and said, "But she be so quiet, Father!" It seemed so lame, but it was all I could think of. And he said that maybe we could help her out of her quietness, and I knew there was some unspoken part to what he had said. I think it be that she could help my Father. But we spoke no more on it.

I know that it is difficult for a man or a woman to be alone in this New World. A man can be a widower in Leyden and a woman can be a widow and be fine, but not really here, not with winter coming and all. Maybe I shall get used to her quietness or maybe she'll become more noisy, but the fact of the matter is she doesn't say tsk-tsk any more.

Love, Mem

September 20, 1621
Plimoth Settlement

Dear Imp,

Mistress Potts has been by every day since Father has been gone on the expedition. She is good with Blessing. There is nothing much else to write. I should have a lot to say when Father and Squanto return.

Love, Mem

September 21, 1621
Plimoth Settlement

D ear Imp,

I could just spit at Mistress Billington. Do you know what she said, and within earshot of Hannah Potts? She said that the only reason my father be drawn to Mistress Potts is for the feather mattress she owns. It is the only real mattress in the settlement and it is filled with down as Mistress Potts' father was a fowler in Leyden and did keep many geese. Well, it was the meanest thing I ever did hear and, poor Hannah, her eyes filled with tears, and I thought she was like to break out crying right there on the spot. So I said to Mistress Billington, "Mind your tongue. My father is pleased by Mistress Potts because she has comely ways and she is dear with Blessing and she makes a nice pudding and she is quiet and elegant in her manner unlike yourself!" And then I just took hold of Hannah's hand, gave her a yank, and we stomped off.

Will the Bilgewaters ever cease to amaze and confound me, Imp?

Love, Mem

September 23, 1621
Plimoth Settlement

Dear Imp,

Father returned last night, and to tell you the truth I have never seen Hannah Potts so animated. She brought her stool over to our house so we could listen by the fire to his stories.

Father said the fields and surrounding lands up there were indeed superior to those here and that many regretted that we had not pushed on. Once there they encountered many Indians, and the women, or squaws, wore cloaks of the most beautiful beaver fur they had yet seen. The women were more than willing to sell their coats for a few handfuls of bright beads and a ribbon or two. So now Father says the fur trade has begun in earnest and he is quite hopeful as to our being able to fulfill our obligations with the merchants.

They actually expect the new ship to be sailing in here fairly soon. I will not think if Hummy by some miracle be on it, for it would have to be a miracle.

But here is another wonderful thing that Father told

us. My heart beats faster just thinking of it. He described to us that at the mouth of the harbour there were many islands and ledges and the men took to naming them. A small cluster at the entrance to the harbour was named the Brewsters in honour of our Ruling Elder. A point of land was named Allerton and guess what, another that rose from the sea so green and lovely and round was named Grace after dear Mam. It was Father's idea. They had wanted to name it Whipple, but Father said no. He wanted it to be called Grace, just Grace. I know now that he still loves her so deeply, but even more important I know now that to the north there is a green and lovely place rising from these bleak and roiling waters named for Mam.

This was a very nice evening. We all – Blessing, me, Father and Hannah – sat close to the fire. Hannah and I were on our stools and when Blessing whined for a turn to sit Father said, "No, Blessing. The stools are for the ladies."

Love, Mem

Dear Imp,

Father and Hannah Potts were married yesterday. Governor Bradford read the service in the large room of the fort. That is where we now have all of our meetings whether they be for making peace treaties with the Indians or worshipping our Lord. It was a very simple wedding. No high merriment or garlands of flowers. Love Brewster helped me braid some wheat sheaves into which we wove some lavender. Wheat is for good luck and fertility. I wouldn't mind another baby about. And it would cheer Mistress Potts something considerable after having lost hers. And we did make a circle of birch leaves and rosemary for the bride's head. Love had brought some tansy for it but I could not bring myself to weave yellow into this wreath. It reminded me too much of Mam and how she did love yellow.

I have no idea what I am to call Hannah Potts. Do I call her Mistress Potts? Stepmother Potts? I cannot call her Mam. If putting tansy in a wreath for her head was too difficult you can imagine, Imp, what calling her Mam would do to me. I'll think on this one a while. I don't think Mistress Potts will be much help. She is still as quiet as a stone and it was all she could do to answer Governor Bradford with "I will" during the ceremony.

Love, Mem

October 10, 1621
Plimoth Settlement

Dear Imp,

We have worked so hard during this harvest season, but praise be to the Lord for indeed with God's blessing we now shall have for each family a peck of meal a week as well as the same in corn for each family. My hands and fingers are sheathed in calluses from shucking all the corn. We had sown some twenty acres with Indian corn and all of it did excellently. We sowed six acres with peas and barley. The peas were a miserable failure. Peas should be sown earlier, for the summers are much hotter here. These came up and blossomed but then were terribly parched by the sun.

Tomorrow be the first morning, except of course for Sabbaths, in over three months when I do not have to rise before the moon is down and the stars swallowed to go work in the fields. What will my fingers do with no corn to shuck? But the harvest is in.

Love, Mem

October 11, 1621
Plimoth Settlement

Dear Imp,

I do indeed think that Governor William Bradford is one of the cleverest men ever. He has declared that we shall have a special time of rejoicing for the gathering of the fruits of our labours! And it is not to last simply one day, or two, but three whole days. Squanto is sent to invite Massasoit and his people. We shall have feasting and entertainments! Four men have already been sent out to get fowl; others to hunt deer; and my father, with John Alden and Masters Winslow and Billington, are sent in the shallop to catch bass and cod and perhaps some eels. Governor Bradford dispatches men with all the skill of Myles Standish drilling and ordering his militia about. I think in truth this is the genius of William Bradford: He can plan celebrations with as much cunning as he can make laws or treaties or compacts. This takes a special kind of mind, I do believe.

Love, Mem

October 13, 1621
Plimoth Settlement

Dear Imp,

Mistress Potts (I still don't know what to call her) and I have, I believe, worked as hard for this feast as we did in the fields. All the women have been cooking from dawn to dusk. Meat stews, fish soups. Squanto has shown me a new dish to make called succotash with a mixture of beans and corn. I promise to make pudding. Father and the men in the shallop did well. They brought in baskets brimming with fish. But Father said Master Billington did little to help. He complained of a sore shoulder and could not haul the nets. So he spent most of his time drinking beer and basking in this October sunshine.

Mistress Billington did not shirk, however, and she was quite helpful to me with the succotash. She apparently has either forgotten or forgiven how sharply I spoke to her. I think it is probably forgotten, not that she is incapable of forgiving. It is just that I don't think anything lasts that long in her mind.

Love, Mem

October 14, 1621
Plimoth Settlement

Dear Imp,

'Tis the first day of the festivities. Massasoit has brought with him 90 Indians. We are busily cooking more. It is so exciting. The whole village bustles and everywhere Indians! The men have their faces painted deep red and they smoke their long pipes – and sometimes the women smoke the pipes, too! The air is laced with the scents of roasting meats and herbs. There are to be games and someone, I think it be Stephen Hopkins, has unearthed a pipe and drum and we ladies get to have a jigging match! I might not be writing much as there is so much to do and so much fun to be had. I'll try just to write for a minute or two, Imp. Fear not I shall never forget you.

Love, Mem

October 15, 1621
Plimoth Settlement

Dear Imp,

I thought I had eaten to the top yesterday, but here I be back for more at the table today. It has been a marvellous time. Mistress Billington jigged until she nearly swooned, but she never let up until finally, in

173

fact, she did collapse. Her cheeks were as red as the lobsters the Indians cooked in the kettle. I had never tasted lobster. It is my favourite. But you must wrestle with it to get the meat out of the claws. Johnny and Francis Billington made themselves lobster moustaches from the thread-like orange tentacles. 'Twas very funny.

Love, Mem

October 17, 1621
Plimoth Settlement

Dear Imp,

The Indians did a most lovely and haunting dance at our festivities. It was full of quietness and we could only hear their soft humming and the click of their beads and their clam-shell necklaces. It is called the deer dance and they do it this time of year, for soon they shall hunt in earnest for the deer. I am not feeling so well tonight. I am not sure I shall join the jigging match.

Love, Mem

November 6, 1621
Plimoth Settlement

Dear Imp,

Finally I awoke and when I did I hardly knew what
had become of me. But, Dear Imp, you and I nearly
parted company. Indeed, I nearly parted company
with everything and everybody on earth. I have
apparently lain at death's doorway for almost three
weeks. My last recollection was wondering if I felt
well enough to go to the jigging match. I would not
have known that if I had not read the page I had
written to you that day. When my father came into our
house he found me sprawled on the floor. My eyes
rolled back in my head, my breath but a dim pulse.

Since that time they, Hannah and he, have nursed
me. I have been bled once by the doctor, and Squanto
came and they gave me teas made with powder of lily
roots, just what I saw them diving for. But I have no
recollection of taking that decoction at all.

Then yesterday morning I heard this lovely voice
singing – singing a song about a faraway stream and I

think in my confused state that I have perhaps died and gone to heaven and this is the voice of an angel. I am so weak I cannot even open my eyes. And I think, yes, truly I be in a heavenly place for I have this feeling of softness and warmth all about me. So I open my eyes, curious to see what heaven looks like. And what do I see but Mistress Hannah Potts and what do I feel but her feather mattress under me and her down coverlet over me. She hath given me her own bed, the one she shares with Father, while I have been ill all these long days. And I move my mouth to speak, but it is I who makes a tsking sound now. So I try again and I say, "Hannah!" And she stops her sweet singing and cries for my father. And so I now know what to call her. She shall always be Hannah to me.

Love, Mem

November 7, 1621
Plimoth Settlement

Dear Imp,

I feel much stronger today. There is talk that the next ship sent by the merchants shall be arriving soon. I try not to think about if Hummy might be on it. But it is hard.

Love, Mem

November 8, 1621
Plimoth Settlement

Dear Imp,

Today I walked. Tomorrow I hope to walk further. I wonder, if indeed the ship would come in, if I could walk to the hill where I saw the *Mayflower* leave with Hummy. For now, as then, I would prefer to watch it all from a grand distance. I know she will not be on it. I know I shall cry either way, if she were or were not. I like to do my crying away from people. You understand, Imp, don't you?

Love, Mem

PS Do you think that there be the slightest possibility that she be coming?

November 10, 1621
Plimoth Settlement

Dear Imp,

The ship has been spotted on the horizon! I am going to the hill. I think I am strong enough, but I shall have to sneak out of the house to do it. They shall soon be going to a meeting in the fort to discuss matters concerning the new arrivals. I shall leave then. I shall take you with me.

Later this same day

Dear Imp,

I have made it. It took me for ever and every breath of wind. My legs do feel like jelly even though I brought Father's eeling staff with me. A chill wind blows but I am bundled well. I now sit in the exact spot I did eight long months ago. I keep telling myself I know Hummy will not be on that ship and yet you cannot kill hope. I think to myself perhaps there shall be another girl like me on the ship to become my friend. But I don't believe this either. You see, I think that true friends when lost are hard to replace.

There is much to hope for even beyond friends, however. I can hope that perhaps a new baby will come into our lives, but maybe not too soon, for Hannah and I have plans for our garden next year. Hannah is still so set to get a big patch of peas to grow. All that will require great strength and much energy. And even if this ship does not carry Hummy it carries much that we need. More tools and things for building, so our little community will grow and, perhaps if there is enough of these things, Father says we shall be able to add on a small room to our house. But then I believe we might have to take away from the garden. So I am not sure which would be best.

They also say that on the next ship that comes there might be spinning wheels and once more we can spin but, better than spinning wheels, there might be chickens and pigs and milk cows!! Oh, I do quiver at the thought of eggs and milk for then truly we can make bag puddings and cakes. Hannah knows how to make ginger cake and she doth have some ginger. Hannah is an excellent baker. Last night when we were talking I said imagine Plimoth growing so that one day there be a bakery just like the ones back in Holland! "And you and I shall be the bakers, Hannah!"

Well, everyone laughed for it is hard to imagine our little settlement ever having shops and the like. 'Tis only a settlement here, after all, but I can imagine a place in the New World, perhaps not as grand as Leyden but a village with winding streets, lined with houses crammed one against the other and signs hanging out over the doors for bakeries and shoe-makers and barrel makers and pickled-fish shops and ribbon shops.

So right now as I watch that ship coming towards our harbour it is a ship of dreams in a way and I look at it and I can dream once again of ginger cake and sweet buns and hope for a new friend and I shall, of course, never give up hoping for Hummy.

If Hummy doesn't come I tell myself it will not be the end of the world. No, I thought the world had ended for two days in April. I thought it would always be winter in my mind. But a thaw has begun inside me. I have after all learned to plant a seed in a hole and bring up corn! I have learned how to beat a stream in the moonlight till it gives forth eels for our cooking pots. I have learned many words in the strange tongue of the Wampanoag. And now here's what I have left to do: I must learn to set a snare for a deer, for I do not like shooting any better than stitchery. I must learn to swim and dive for lily roots with two sets of petticoats on. I must some day learn to sail and then on that day I shall set a course for an island that rises out of the sea all green and lovely that is called Grace.

For what I have learned and what I hope to learn, for all of this I give thanks.

Love, Mem

Epilogue

Many of Remember's hopes and dreams came true, others did not. She never again saw her dear friend Humility Sawyer, and Mem's and Hannah's plans for peas and a bigger garden did not succeed, nor did the dreams of abundant crops come true for the rest of the settlement.

In 1628, when Mem was nineteen years old she married William Endicott.

In 1630, the city of Boston was founded and Mem and her husband moved there along with others who realized that their destiny was not to try and tame the backbreaking, rock-strewn New England soil.

Soon after, Mem gave birth to twin girls whom she named Humility and Grace. Her husband, William, became a successful merchant of dried fish and soon branched out into lumbering. Many others from the original Plimoth settlement found their way to Boston, including Blessing who married a cousin of William Endicott's, and finally Hannah came as a widow when Mem's father died.

Mem and Hannah and Mem's twins along with Blessing and Hannah's two young sons by Mem's father baked hardtack and sea biscuits for the larders of ships in the merchant trade. But they also baked cinnamon buns and Hannah Potts Whipple's special ginger cake, which could not go to sea, but became famous in many homes.

Remember Patience Whipple lived a very long life. So long that the best dream of all was fulfilled. She lived to see her children's children's children. And in fact it was a great-great-great-granddaughter, a Miss Humility Albright, who discovered the diary of Remember Patience Whipple Endicott in a trunk blackened with age in the attic of her parents' house on Beacon Hill in Boston in the year 1850.

Historical Note

In 1620, the Pilgrims sailed to America in order to escape religious and political persecution and establish a settlement where they could live and worship in a way that they defined as godly.

In their native England under King James I's reign, the Church of England was very powerful. Anyone who did not follow the established religion or co-operate with the King's wishes faced persecution, in the form of arrests, imprisonment, fines and other types of official harassment.

A group of reformers called Puritans questioned the church's power and a faction of them began to condemn the church as corrupt and unlawful. They were scorned by the King because their questioning threatened his authority as well as that of the church. Some of them began to meet in secret. They were known as Separatists because they wanted to separate themselves completely from the church. When the King found out about their meetings, some Separatists were sentenced to jail. Two had already been hanged.

In 1607, a group of them decided they could no longer live in a country where the practice of religion was forced on people under threat of arrest.

For fear of their livelihoods as well as their lives, the Separatists decided to move to Leyden, Holland, where they could worship freely. But life in Holland was hard economically and they felt extremely isolated in this new land. They were also worried that their children would forget how to speak English or become soldiers and sailors for Holland.

They decided to emigrate to the New World. These Separatists came to be known as Pilgrims. They were led by the wise elder, William Brewster, and an idealistic young man named William Bradford. The Pilgrims knew that another English colony had already been established in Jamestown, Virginia, in 1607, and they were ready to create their own colony in Northern Virginia.

They were able to convince some London businessmen, the Merchant Adventurers, to sponsor their voyage. In return for financial backing by the London group, the Pilgrims promised to work for the next seven years to pay off their debts. Essentially, they would be indentured servants to this coalition of merchants, who hoped to accumulate a great profit from their chartered colony. The Pilgrims returned to England where they were provided with a small wooden ship named the *Mayflower* and some supplies to help them survive their first months in the wilds of America.

On Wednesday, September 6, 1620, 102 brave people, including 34 children, crowded onto the ship and set off to form a colony of their own. About 35 of them were going for religious reasons – they were the Pilgrims (though they preferred to call themselves Saints) – others because they couldn't find work in England, and still others for the spirit of adventure.

The journey was long and difficult. There was little to eat except for salted beef and pork, dry biscuits and also some cheese, peas and beans from Holland. But food spoiled quickly and the barrelled water was not safe to drink. Many of the passengers were terribly seasick, and two (including one sailor) died during the gruelling trip. After more than two months, the Pilgrims arrived at what is now Cape Cod, Massachusetts. Since they had been planning to settle in Virginia Colony, it was clear that they had gone more than a little off course.

Cape Cod looked to be a rocky and ominous land. After determining to explore further, the Pilgrims sailed inland to the more welcoming shores of Plymouth, which had been discovered and named six years earlier by Captain John Smith. On December 21, 1620, the Pilgrims finally stepped ashore. No one is quite sure whether any of the Pilgrims actually stepped on the rock now known as Plymouth Rock, but many people believe the legend developed because it was the only good landing place along two and a half miles of beach.

The first few months in Plymouth were cold and harsh for the new immigrants. Coming to this foreign land in the dead of winter was probably not the best plan. The Pilgrims arrived with no shelter, no medical care and very few provisions. And because they still had to build houses, many of them spent most of the winter living aboard the ship. Illness swept through the tiny community, and more than half the Pilgrims died during that first winter. Some were killed by starvation and scurvy, while others died from pneumonia, fevers and other diseases. While the Pilgrims did use medicinal herbs, there was no medicine that could cure the ravaging diseases that were killing them. Many doctors believed in bleeding ill patients, opening a vein to let some "poisoned" blood flow out.

The Pilgrims had agreed to elect a man named John Carver to be their first governor, but he did not survive the long winter. William Bradford was elected to take his place. He and the other leaders of the group created a document called the Mayflower Compact, signed by all of the men in the small colony. In it, they agreed to hold annual elections for a governor and assistants, who would draft fair laws for all to follow. While America's struggle for independence was over 150 years away, the early seeds of self-government were sown by the Pilgrims.

The Plymouth colonists came in almost immediate contact with the Indian peoples. Some of the local tribes, like the various Wampanoag groups, were friendly toward the Pilgrims. The Wampanoag had been trading furs with European traders for years before the *Mayflower* landed, but the Pilgrims were the first Europeans to settle permanently on Wampanoag land.

On March 16, 1621, three months after their arrival, the Pilgrims met an Abenaki Indian named Samoset who spoke English and told them all about the neighbouring Indian tribes. He also introduced them to another Indian named Tisquantum, or Squanto, the only surviving Patuxet native of Plymouth. He became their dearest friend and stayed with the Pilgrims for the rest of his life. When spring came and the Pilgrims were able to plant their first crops, Squanto introduced them to maize, or Indian corn. He also taught the Pilgrims how to fish and where to hunt for deer and turkey. While some of the English crops like beans and wheat did not grow very well in the rocky New England soil, maize thrived. The Pilgrims traded their surplus corn to the Indians for beaver pelts. These furs were then sent to England to help pay off their debts.

There were other tribes, like the Gayhead and the Narrangansetts, who were not as welcoming to the Pilgrims, and Captain Miles Standish helped form a militia, providing self-defence for the fledgling community.

That October, the surviving Pilgrims (about 50) celebrated the first Thanksgiving. It lasted three days, and they invited members of the Wampanoag tribe to join them for the joyful feast. They ate wild turkey, deer, meat pies, duck, fresh fish, vegetables from the Pilgrims' gardens, corn and wild berries. The Pilgrims had much to be thankful for. Without the help of Squanto and their Indian neighbours, they would not have survived their first year. They also signed an official peace treaty with the Wampanoag chief,

Massasoit. Later, the British would take advantage of the Pilgrims' new allies and force them to move away from their ancestral lands, but this did not happen initially.

For the next few years, the Pilgrims were almost isolated in their new settlement. Their population grew slowly, as every so often, ships would arrive from England with some new immigrants. For the most part, though, the Pilgrims were on their own.

The company of London never made a profit from the Pilgrims. It was too hard to exert control over colonies that were so far away. Plymouth was now essentially independent, although the King of England still had final jurisdiction over their activities. In practice, the Pilgrims were a self-governing community, but their fight for independence was only just beginning.

Timeline

1603–1625 Reign of James I.

1605 The Gunpowder Plot.

1607 Jamestown, Virginia, is founded.

1611 The King James' Bible is produced.

1616 Tobacco is first exported from Virginia.

1620 *Mayflower* lands at Plymouth, Massachusetts.

1621 The first Thanksgiving.

1625–1649 Reign of Charles I.

1625 The population of the English colonies in America reaches 2,000.

1642–1649 English Civil War.

1649 King Charles I is beheaded.

1649–1660 The Commonwealth and Protectorate in England.

1660 The English monarchy is restored under King Charles II.

1665 The Great Plague in London.

1666 The Great Fire of London.

1685–1688 Reign of James II.

1692 Witch trials at Salem, Massachusetts.

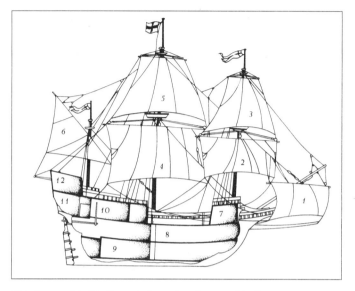

This diagram of the Mayflower *indicates the main areas of the ship.*

1. *Spiritsail*
2. *Forecourse*
3. *Fore-topsail*
4. *Main course*
5. *Main-topsail*
6. *Mizzen sail*
7. *Fo'c'sle (Where meals were cooked for the crew.)*
8. *'Tween decks (living quarters)*
9. *Hold (storage for food, drink, tools and supplies.)*
10. *Steerage (This is where the helmsman steered the ship. He guided the whipstaff, the long lever that moved the tiller, which moved the rudder. An officer on the deck above the steerage gave the orders.)*
11. *Great cabin (The ship's master, some of the officers and the ship's apprentice slept here.)*
12. *Round house (The chartroom from which the master directed the ship's course.)*

The names of those which came ouer first, in y̆ year 1620.
and were (by the blesing of God) the first begiñers, and
(in a sort) the foundation, of all the plantations, and
Colonies, in Nem-England (And their families)

mͬ John Caruer.
kathrine his wife·
Desire minter; &
·2· man-seruants
John Howland
Roger :wilder·
william Latham, a boy.
& a maid seruant & a
Child y̆ was put to him
called, Jasper More

8

mͬ William Brewster.
Mary his wife, with
·2 sons, whose names
were Loue, & wrasling
and a boy was put to
him called Richard More, and another
the rest of his Children of his Brothers
were left behind & came
ouer afterwards·

6

mͬ Edward Winslow
Elizabeth his wife, &
2 men seruants, caled
georg Sowle, and
Elias Story; also a litle
girle was put to him caled
Ellen, the sister of Richard
More·

5

william Bradford. and
Doraty his wife, hauing
but one Child, a sone left
behind, who came afterward.

2

mͬ Isaack Allerton, and
Mary ·his wife; with ·3· Children
Bartholomew
Remember, &
Mary· and a seruant boy,
John Hooke·

6

mͬ Samuell fuller; and
a seruant · caled
William Button· His wife
was behind & a Child, which
came afterwards·

2

John Crackston and his sone
John Crackston

2

Captin myles Standish
and Rose, his wife

2

mͬ Christopher martin,
and his wife; and ·2· seruants,
Salamon prower, and
John Langemore

4

mͬ William Mullines, and his
wife; and ·2· Children
Joseph, & priscila; and a seruant
Robart Carter·

5

mͬ William White, and
Susana his wife, and one sone
Caled rdsolued, and one borne
a ship-bord caled perigriene; &
·2· seruants, named
William Holbeck, & Edward Thomson

6

mͬ Steuen Hopkins, &
Elizabeth his wife; and ·2·
Children, caled giles, and
Constanta a doughter, both
by a former wife. And ·2· more
by this wife, caled Damaris, &
Oceanus, the last was borne at
sea. And ·2· seruants, called
Edward Doty, and Edward Litster

8

mͬ Richard Warren, but his
wife and Children were lefte
behind and came afterwards

1

John Billington, and Elen his wife·
and ·2· sones John & francis·

4

Edward Tillie, and Ann his wife·
and ·2· Children that were their·
Cosens; Henery Samson, and Humil·
lity Coper

4

John Tillie, and his wife; and
Eelizabeth their doughter

3

A roster of signatures of some of the people on the Mayflower.

193

The city of Leyden, Holland, was much more developed than the rugged landscape that awaited the Pilgrims on the shores of New England.

The Pilgrims worked together to build their first homes. They modelled them on their houses in England, only much smaller. They had thatched roofs, and windows often covered with oiled paper to let in some light.

Plymouth Colony after the Pilgrims had built their homes.

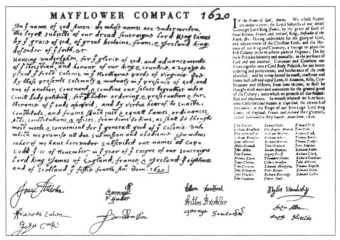

Forty-one men signed the Mayflower Compact, which promised "just and equall lawes for the general good of all". It was the first document in America based on majority rule.

The Pilgrims' long woollen dresses and white linen caps were different from the dress of the native peoples they encountered.

An artist's interpretation of the First Thanksgiving, which took place sometime in the middle of October, 1621. It lasted for three days.

PSALME 100.

Howt to Iehovah , all the earth. 2.

Serve ye Iehovah with gladnes: before
K 3 him

him come with finging-merth. Know

that Iehovah he God *is*:

Itts he *that* made us, and not wee;
his folk, and fheep of his feeding.
O with confeffion enter yee
his gates, his courtyards with praifing:
  Confefs to him, blefs ye his name.
Becaufe Iehovah *he* good *is*:
his mercy ever *is the fame*:
and his faith, unto all ages.

Psalm 100, a favourite Pilgrim hymn, from The Book of Psalms.

197

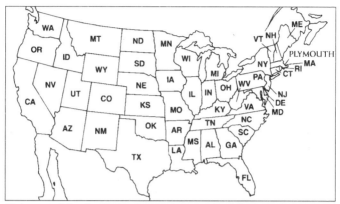

Modern map of America showing the approximate location of Plymouth.

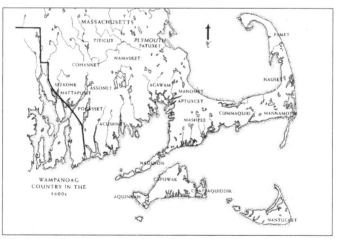

This detail of Massachusetts shows Plymouth, which the Indians called Patuxet. Also shown are the neighbouring areas with their place names as they were known in the 1600s.

Picture acknowledgments

The Hunger
The Diary of Phyllis McCormack,
Ireland 1845-1847

Voyage on the Great Titanic
The Diary of Margaret Anne Brady, 1912

Blitz
The Diary of Edie Benson,
London 1940-41

Twentieth-Century Girl
The Diary of Flora Bonnington,
London 1899-1900

My Story.

Transported
The Diary of Elizabeth Harvey,
Australia 1790

Mill Girl
The Diary of Eliza Helsted,
Manchester 1842-1843

Bloody Tower
The Diary of Tilly Middleton,
London 1553-1559

Civil War
Thomas Adamson
England 1643-1650

Trafalgar
James Grant
HMS Norseman 1799-1806

The Trenches
Billy Stevens
The Western Front 1914-1918

Battle of Britain
Harry Woods
England 1939-1941

Armada
Thomas Hobbs
England 1587-1588

Crimea
Michael Pope
110th Regiment 1853-1857

Indian Mutiny
Hanuman Singh
India 1857-1858

Zulu War
Jabulani
Africa 1879-1882